World Geography Puzzles

EDITOR: MARY A. DIETERICH

COPYRIGHT © 2010 Mark Twain Media, Inc.

ISBN 978-1-58037-559-7

Printing No. CD-404133

Mark Twain Media, Inc., Publishers
Distributed by Carson-Dellosa Publishing LLC

Visit us at www.carsondellosa.com

The purchase of this book entitles the buyer to reproduce the student pages for classroom use only. Other permissions may be obtained by writing Mark Twain Media, Inc., Publishers.

All rights reserved. Printed in the United States of America.

Table of Contents

Introduction 1

Maps 2

Latitude and Longitude 4

Earth's Hemispheres and Continents 6

Earth's Seasons 8

Day and Night on Earth 10

Earth's Wind Belts 12

Ocean Currents 14

Cultures From Around the World 16

Location 18

Place 20

Human-Environment Interaction 22

Movement 24

Regions 26

North America
    Locations of Major Cities 28
    Physical Features 29
    Plants, Animals, and Resources 30
    Native Americans 31
    Regions 33

South America
    Locations of Major Cities 34
    Physical Features 35
    Plants, Animals, and Resources 36
    Colonial Settlement 37
    Regions 39

Europe
    Locations of Major Cities 40
    Physical Features 41
    Plants, Animals, and Resources 42
    Movement of People, Goods, and
        Ideas 43
    Regions 45

Africa
    Locations of Major Cities 46
    Physical Features 47
    Plants, Animals, and Resources 48
    Climate 49
    Regions of Conflict 51

Asia
    Locations of Major Cities 52
    Physical Features 53
    Plants, Animals, and Resources 55
    Population Density 56
    Regions 57

Australia and Oceania
    Locations of Major Cities 58
    Physical Features 59
    Plants, Animals, and Resources 60
    Movement of Early People and
        Culture 61
    Regions 64

Antarctica
    Location 65
    Physical Features 66
    Plants and Animals 67
    Exploration 68
    International Agreements and
        Possible Resources 69

Answer Keys 71

Bibliography 78

Introduction

World Geography Puzzles provides students with a variety of fun and challenging puzzles and activities designed to reinforce geography concepts. Reading selections are followed by crossword, word search, word scramble, decoding, and last letter/first letter puzzles. Students gain practice and reinforcement of vocabulary, spelling, and reading comprehension skills as they solve puzzles and complete word games. They also learn valuable geography concepts, such as map reading, latitude and longitude, what makes days and seasons, how winds and ocean currents circulate around the earth, and how people of other cultures live.

Depending on the skill level of the students, teachers may want to provide a word list for puzzles that do not already have them. Finding the latitude and longitude coordinates for locations can also be an optional, extra credit activity for some of the puzzles. The different types of puzzles provide a range of activities for students of varying abilities.

Students will also be introduced to the five themes of geography that are used to study the world around us. The themes cover location, place, human-environment interaction, movement, and regions. These themes were developed by the Joint Committee on Geographic Education of the National Council for Geographic Education and the Association of American Geographers.

- **Location:** where things are located on Earth, both in absolute and relative terms

- **Place:** the physical and human characteristics that make a place distinct from all others

- **Human-Environment Interaction:** how the land affects the people and how the people affect the land

- **Movement:** how the movement of natural forces, people, goods, and ideas affect a place

- **Regions:** what common physical and human characteristics link a place to other parts of the world

Each of the seven continents is highlighted in its own section with an emphasis on exploring the five themes. Activities include finding the latitude and longitude coordinates for major cities; identifying physical features; learning about the plants, animals, and resources of each continent; exploring the history, culture, and movements of early peoples; and distinguishing the unique regions of the continents. Students will gain a better understanding of the human and physical geography of their planet as they complete these fun, engaging puzzles.

Maps

Maps are a valuable tool that can help you locate places, plan how to get from one place to another, and see what landforms, climates, or resources are in a certain place. A location can be relative or absolute. A **relative location** is a general description of a place as it relates to other places. For example, the relative location of Houston, Texas, is near the Gulf Coast of Texas, west of Louisiana, and north of Mexico. An **absolute location** is the exact latitude and longitude coordinates on a map or globe. Houston, Texas, is located at 30 degrees North latitude and 95 degrees West longitude (30°N, 95°W).

Whether you are looking for a relative location or an absolute location, there are several features of a map that make it useful. The map may have a grid of **latitude** (horizontal) lines and **longitude** (vertical) lines. These lines provide a specific point for each location. There may also be symbols on the map that indicate where capital cities, rivers, railroads, parks, national monuments, hospitals, airports, and many other things are located. Some maps may use colors to indicate different areas of climate, terrain, vegetation, political division, or population density. Somewhere on the map there should be a **map legend** or **map key** that explains what these symbols and colors mean.

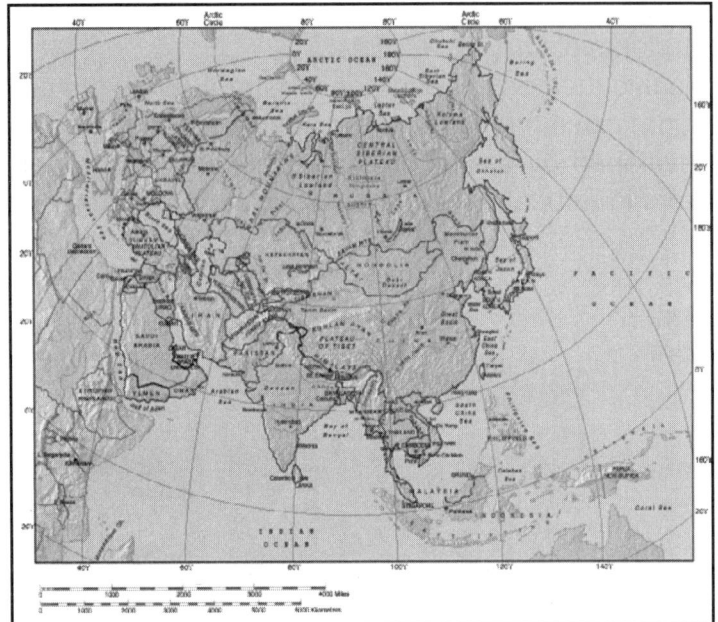

Since a map is a small drawing or representation of an actual place that is much larger, maps are said to be drawn to scale. A map may be one-tenth or one-thousandth the size of the actual place. The **map scale** tells you what the distance on the map is equal to in real life. For example, one inch on a map may be equal to 1,000 miles in real life, or one centimeter may be equal to 250 kilometers. When you use a road map, you can measure the distance between two points and then multiply the distance by the number on the map scale to determine what the distance is in real life.

There are many different types of maps. Each map provides different information. A **physical map** shows the physical features of a place, such as mountains, rivers, and plains. **Topographic maps** show the different elevations of a region. They show how high or low the surface of the earth is by shading each elevation a different color. All the points that are at the same elevation are connected by lines called **contour lines**. When contour lines are close together, it indicates that the land is going steeply up or down. A **political map** shows the different governmental divisions of a place, such as cities, counties, and countries. Road maps and city maps show the highways and streets you need to travel to get from one place to another. There are other types of maps that show the climate, population density, land use, precipitation, and natural resources of a region. In fact, anything you want to know about an area can probably be illustrated with a map.

World Geography Puzzles   Maps

Name: _____ Date: _____

Maps: Crossword Puzzle

Directions: Use the clues below to complete the crossword puzzle. All the words are related to maps.

ACROSS

2. All the points on a map that are at the same elevation are connected by ____ ____.
5. A map that shows the different countries of the world is a ____ map.
7. General description of a place as it relates to other places (two words)
10. Maps are drawn to ____ to represent an actual place that is much larger.
12. Colors on a map may be used to show climate, terrain, ____, political division, or population density.
13. If you want to travel from St. Louis, Missouri, to Atlanta, Georgia, by car, you need a ____ ____ to plan your trip.
14. A map may use ____ to indicate where capital cities, rivers, parks, or hospitals are located.

DOWN

1. ____ maps show how high or low the surface of the earth is by shading each elevation a different color.
2. The specific point on a map indicated by latitude and longitude, such as 30°N, 95°W, is called the map ____.
3. Tells what the distance on a map is equal to in real life (two words)
4. The exact latitude and longitude coordinates on a map or globe (two words)
6. Horizontal lines on a map used to locate a place
8. Vertical lines on a map used to locate a place
9. Explains what the symbols and colors on a map mean (two words)
11. This type of map shows the features of a place, such as mountains, rivers, and plains.

CD-404133 © Mark Twain Media, Inc., Publishers   3

Latitude and Longitude

Places on the surface of the earth can be located using latitude and longitude. Latitude and longitude lines are imaginary lines that form a grid on a globe or map. **Latitude** lines are the horizontal lines that measure distance north and south of the imaginary line called the equator. The **equator** is 0° latitude. Latitude is measured from 0 to 90 degrees north or south of the equator. **Longitude** lines are the vertical lines that measure distance east and west of the imaginary line called the Prime Meridian. The **Prime Meridian** is 0° longitude, and the lines of longitude continue to the opposite side of the globe to 180°. Longitude is measured from 0 to 180 degrees east and west of the Prime Meridian. The **International Date Line** roughly follows the 180° longitude line.

These lines can be used like a coordinate grid to locate a specific point. The latitude coordinate is always given first, and the longitude coordinate is given second. For example, if you are given the coordinates 40°N, 80°W, find the 40° north line of latitude and follow it until you reach 80° west longitude. This location is near Pittsburgh, Pennsylvania. To pinpoint a location even further, coordinates are given in degrees (°), minutes ('), and seconds ("). For example, Pittsburgh is located at 40°26'24"N, 79°59'24"W. Some maps and global positioning systems (GPS) may also write this as decimals: 40.438315°N, 79.997449°W.

Lines of latitude are also called **parallels** because all the lines are parallel to each other. Any line around the earth that divides it into two halves is a **great circle**. The equator is the only line of latitude that is a great circle. The equator divides the earth into the Northern and Southern Hemispheres. The circles formed by the lines of latitude get smaller as they get closer to the North and South Poles. The **North Pole** is at 90° north latitude, and the **South Pole** is at 90° south latitude.

Lines of Latitude

Lines of Longitude

Lines of longitude are also called **meridians**, and they all begin and end at the Poles. These lines are not parallel. Each line of longitude and its opposite on the other side of the earth form a great circle. The great circle formed by the Prime Meridian and 180° longitude divides the earth into the Eastern and Western Hemispheres.

When measuring distance in miles using the number of degrees of latitude between two locations, each degree equals approximately 69 miles. This is a constant because the lines of latitude are parallel. (1° of latitude = 69 miles) When measuring distance in miles using the number of degrees of longitude between two locations, the number of miles for each degree will change, based on the latitude of the two locations. The adjustment in miles for each degree of longitude difference is due to the fact that as the lines of longitude approach the Poles, the distance between the lines decreases. (1° of longitude = 69 miles at 0° latitude; 65 miles at 15° latitude; 60 miles at 30° latitude; 35 miles at 60° latitude)

World Geography Puzzles Latitude and Longitude

Name: _____ Date: _____

Latitude and Longitude: Word Search

Directions: Read the clues below and figure out what words the clues represent. Then find and circle the words in the word search puzzle. Words can go horizontally, vertically, and diagonally in all eight directions. When you are done, the first 51 unused letters in the grid will spell out a hidden message. Pick them out from left to right, top line to bottom line.

```
T H I E L E Q U A T L O R I S P T H E O N
L Y N L I A N E O F L O A T I T O U D E T
H A T T D I B S A G R E N A T C I L R C L
E G E H I N N O F X R N K G F C K N E H H
R C R B R K P Q L N D R W Y I Z M T F S W
B G N C G T R Y R G Y G M J B T S T E Z W
C L A H T M I Q H L D T C V H N U D V V B
J Z T Y H L M N V T T B V K A G U D D R C
K L I K K E C S E T U N I M T P I E K R
N W O L M C M R G Z M V D T I K S V N J V
W H N L M L E F K Z W I N T C T M M L X K
W W A N M F R C W L R J A O A B J K W H M
T K L R N H I V M E M L O N K L M M V X S
W L D L R K D D M V P R C N K R K Z L G L
K R A M P J I M N B D E L G K P K K X J E
B T T H Y M A G T I N E Q U A T O R Q G L
M B E N K R N D N N R E L L A M S B G L L
X Z L P N F X A T G R E A T C I R C L E A
J J I K F N T C N K L R H R L Y M K D N R
J N N R N E G L B N B K N L L Q C R K X A
L M E K H K P D V K J F P T R T M N N C P
```

Word List

1. _____
2. _____
3. _____
4. _____
5. _____
6. _____
7. _____
   _____
8. _____
9. _____
10. _____
11. _____
12. _____
13. _____
14. _____
    _____
15. _____

1. The latitude ____ is always given first, and the longitude coordinate is given second.
2. As lines of longitude approach the Poles, the ____ between the lines decreases.
3. The ____ is 0° latitude.
4. ____ positioning systems may give coordinates as decimals.
5. Any line around the earth that divides it into two halves is a ____ ____.
6. Latitude and longitude lines are imaginary lines that form a ____ on a globe or map.
7. The ____ ____ ____ roughly follows the 180° longitude line.
8. ____ lines are the horizontal lines that measure distance north and south of the imaginary line called the equator.
9. ____ lines are the vertical lines that measure distance east and west of the imaginary line called the Prime Meridian.
10. Lines of longitude are also called ____.
11. Coordinates are given in degrees, ____, and seconds.
12. Lines of latitude are also called ____.
13. All meridians of longitude begin and end at the ____.
14. The ____ ____ is 0° longitude.
15. The circles formed by the lines of latitude get ____ as they get closer to the North and South Poles.

CD-404133 © Mark Twain Media, Inc., Publishers

Earth's Hemispheres and Continents

The word **hemisphere** means "half of a globe." *Hemi* means "half," and *sphere* means "ball or globe." The earth is a sphere, and a globe is a model of the earth.

The earth is divided into four hemispheres. The equator at 0° latitude divides the earth into the Northern and Southern Hemispheres. Everything from 0° to 90° north is the **Northern Hemisphere**. Everything from 0° to 90° south is the **Southern Hemisphere**. The great circle formed by the Prime Meridian at 0° longitude and the International Date Line at 180° longitude divides the earth into the Eastern and Western Hemispheres. Everything from 0° to 180° east is the **Eastern Hemisphere**. Everything from 0° to 180° west is the **Western Hemisphere**.

Continents are the large landmasses on Earth's surface that are completely or mostly surrounded by water. At one time, all the continents may have been together in one landmass that scientists have called **Pangaea**. As this landmass broke up, these plates of the earth's surface began to move apart slowly. The theory of **Plate Tectonics** suggests that these plates move a few inches each year. In some places the plates are moving apart, while in others they are colliding or scraping against each other. This accounts for volcano and earthquake activity, mountain formation, and undersea trench and mountain formation.

In order to locate a place on a map or globe, we use the coordinate system of latitude and longitude. The most basic information we can get from this system is in which hemisphere a place is located. The continents of North America, Europe, and Asia (except for a few islands) are located completely in the Northern Hemisphere. Australia and Antarctica are located completely in the Southern Hemisphere. South America and Africa are divided by the equator, so they have land in both the Northern and Southern Hemispheres. North America and South America are completely in the Western Hemisphere. Australia is completely in the Eastern Hemisphere. Almost all of Asia is in the Eastern Hemisphere. Only a small area of Russia extends into the Western Hemisphere. Most of Europe and Africa are in the Eastern Hemisphere, but they are crossed by the Prime Meridian, so some of their land is in the Western Hemisphere. Antarctica is divided by the Prime Meridian and the International Date Line, with the larger part of its actual land area in the Eastern Hemisphere.

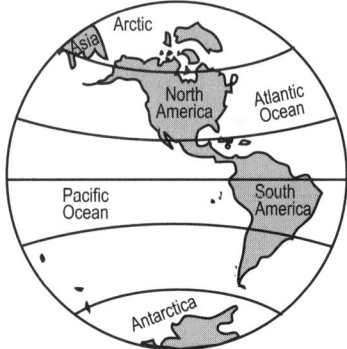
Western Hemisphere

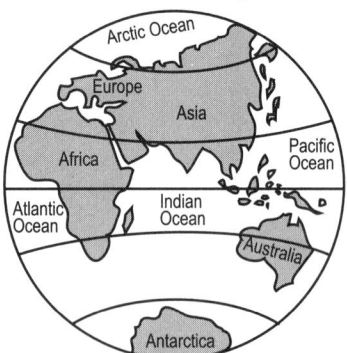
Eastern Hemisphere

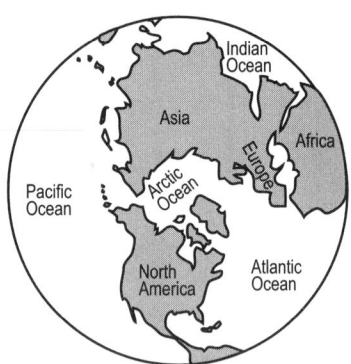
Northern Hemisphere

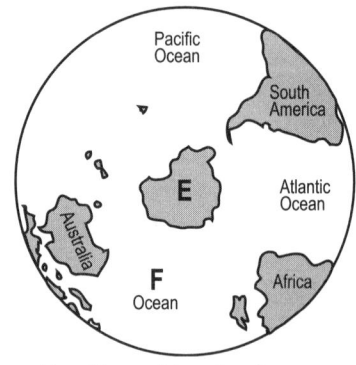
Southern Hemisphere

World Geography Puzzles Earth's Hemispheres and Continents

Name: _____ Date: _____

Earth's Hemispheres and Continents: Matching

Directions: Use an atlas, globe, or online maps to find the following places. Then write the letter of the correct hemisphere on the blank next to the place. Some places may be associated with more than one hemisphere.

E. Eastern Hemisphere
N. Northern Hemisphere
W. Western Hemisphere
S. Southern Hemisphere

_____ 1. Asia

_____ 2. Africa

_____ 3. North America

_____ 4. Australia

_____ 5. South America

_____ 6. Antarctica

_____ 7. Europe

_____ 8. Argentina

_____ 9. Ukraine

_____ 10. Japan

_____ 11. Canada

_____ 12. New Zealand

_____ 13. Liberia

_____ 14. Finland

_____ 15. Kenya

_____ 16. China

_____ 17. Bolivia

_____ 18. Mexico

_____ 19. Algeria

_____ 20. Greece

_____ 21. Brazil

_____ 22. Indonesia

_____ 23. Afghanistan

_____ 24. Honduras

_____ 25. Chile

_____ 26. Democratic Republic of Congo

_____ 27. United States

_____ 28. Great Britain

_____ 29. Colombia

_____ 30. Iraq

_____ 31. Ghana

_____ 32. Italy

_____ 33. Red Sea

_____ 34. Hudson Bay

_____ 35. Weddell Sea

_____ 36. Lake Baikal

_____ 37. Caribbean Sea

_____ 38. Lake Victoria

_____ 39. Rocky Mountains

_____ 40. Great Barrier Reef

Earth's Seasons

As Earth travels around the sun in the course of a year (365 1/4 days), it experiences different seasons: spring, summer, fall or autumn, and winter. Areas of the earth receive differing amounts and intensities of sunlight at different times of the year, so each season is associated with different temperatures, weather, and plant growth. These differences are more noticeable the farther away from the equator you get.

The seasons occur at opposite times of the year in the Northern and Southern Hemispheres. In the Northern Hemisphere **spring** begins about March 21, **summer** begins about June 21, **fall** begins about September 21, and **winter** begins about December 21. While the Northern Hemisphere is having summer, the Southern Hemisphere is having winter, and so on. The first day of spring is called the **vernal equinox**, and the first day of fall is called the **autumnal equinox** because these days have equal amounts of daylight and darkness. The first day of summer is called the **summer solstice**. This day has the most hours of daylight in the year. The first day of winter is called the **winter solstice**. It has the fewest hours of daylight in the year.

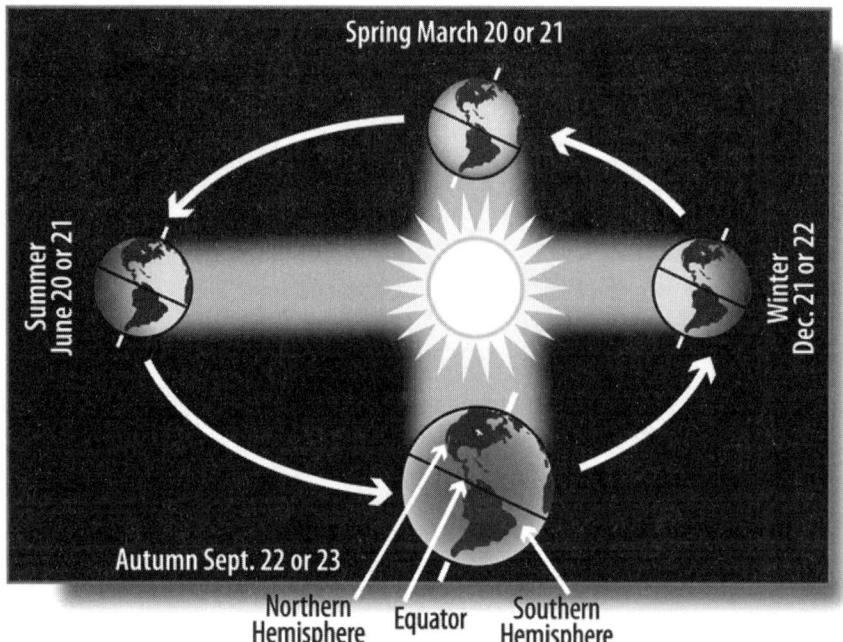

What causes these seasons? It is because the earth travels around, or **revolves** around, the sun and also because the earth is tilted on its axis at 23 1/2 degrees. Because the earth is tilted as it travels around the sun, sometimes the Northern Hemisphere is pointed more toward the sun, and sometimes the Southern Hemisphere is pointed more toward the sun. Whichever hemisphere is pointed toward the sun receives more direct sunlight and more hours of sunlight each day. This is the summer season, and it allows for warmer temperatures and good growing conditions for plants. When a hemisphere is pointed away from the sun, it receives less direct sunlight and fewer hours of sunlight each day. This is the winter season, which is much colder. During the spring and fall seasons, the sunlight strikes the earth more evenly, so there is not much difference in the Northern and Southern Hemisphere temperatures. Locations along the equator do not experience much difference in seasons because sunlight is always shining directly at the equator.

The shape of earth's orbit around the sun is called an **ellipse**. It looks like an elongated circle. Because of the shape of the orbit, the earth is closer to the sun at certain points in the orbit, and at other points, it is farther away. However, this difference in distance does not have as much impact on seasons as the tilt of the earth.

World Geography Puzzles   Earth's Seasons

Name: _____ Date: _____

Earth's Seasons: Decoding

Directions: Decode the missing words in the text below by using the code key at the bottom of the page.

1. The differences in seasons are more noticeable the farther away from the __ __ __ __ __ __ __ you get.
   _{22 10 6 26 7 12 9}

2. The seasons occur at opposite times of the year in the Northern and Southern __ __ __ __ __ __ __ __ __ __.
   _{19 22 14 18 8 11 19 22 9 22 8}

3. The Northern Hemisphere __ __ __ __ __ __ begins about March 21.
   _{8 11 9 18 13 20}

4. The first day of spring is called the __ __ __ __ __ __ __ __ __ __ __ __ __.
   _{5 22 9 13 26 15 22 10 6 18 13 12 3}

5. __ __ __ __ __ __ begins about June 21 in the Northern Hemisphere.
   _{8 6 14 14 22 9}

6. The day with the most hours of daylight is called the summer __ __ __ __ __ __ __ __.
   _{8 12 15 8 7 18 24 22}

7. The first day of fall, about September 21 in the Northern Hemisphere, is called the __ __ __ __ __ __ __ __ equinox.
   _{26 6 7 6 14 13 26 15}

8. Winter in the Northern Hemisphere begins about __ __ __ __ __ __ __ __ 21.
   _{23 22 24 22 14 25 22 9}

9. The day wth the fewest hours of daylight is called the __ __ __ __ __ __ solstice.
   _{4 18 13 7 22 9}

10. Seasons change because the earth __ __ __ __ __ __ __ __ around the sun.
    _{9 22 5 12 15 5 22 8}

11. Because the earth is __ __ __ __ __ __ on its axis, the Northern or Southern Hemisphere is pointed more toward the sun at certain times of the year.
    _{7 18 15 7 22 23}

12. Earth travels around the sun in an orbit shaped like an __ __ __ __ __ __ __.
    _{22 15 15 18 11 8 22}

13. When the Northern Hemisphere is tilted more toward the sun, it is receiving more direct __ __ __ __ __ __ __.
    _{8 6 13 15 18 20 19 7}

14. There is not much difference in seasons near the equator because sunlight is always shining __ __ __ __ __ __ __ __ at this area.
    _{23 18 9 22 24 7 15 2}

15. Each __ __ __ __ __ __ is associated with different temperatures, weather, and plant growth.
    _{8 22 26 8 12 13}

A	B	C	D	E	F	G	H	I	J	K	L	M	N	O	P	Q	R	S	T	U	V	W	X	Y	Z
26	25	24	23	22	21	20	19	18	17	16	15	14	13	12	11	10	9	8	7	6	5	4	3	2	1

Day and Night on Earth

As the earth revolves around the sun, it also **rotates**, or spins, on its **axis**, which is the imaginary line through the center of the earth from north to south. This rotation causes periods of daylight and darkness. The earth rotates from west to east.

The earth makes one complete rotation on its axis every 24 hours. This is called a **day**. Because the earth is divided into 360 degrees of longitude, you can divide 360 by 24 hours to get 15 degrees. So for every hour that passes, the earth moves 15 degrees. The sun (or moon) appears to move in the sky because the earth is rotating at 15 degrees per hour. The dividing line between the part of the earth that is illuminated by sunlight and the part that is not illuminated is called the **terminator**. There is daylight on one side of the line and darkness on the other side. This line moves around the earth at 15 degrees per hour as the earth rotates.

This is why there are **time zones** set up to keep track of the local time on earth. There are 24 time zones that are each approximately 15 degrees of longitude wide. Variations may occur in certain areas as states or countries choose to go with one time zone or another. If it is 12:00 noon at 0° longitude at the **Prime Meridian**, it is 1:00 P.M. at 15°E longitude, and it is 11:00 A.M. at 15°W longitude. This continues until the **International Date Line** is reached at 180°. There it is one date on the east side of the line and another date on the west side of the line.

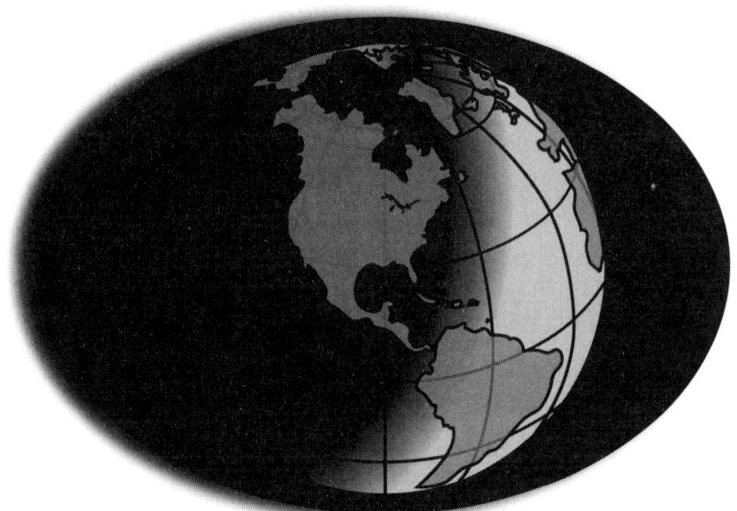

The hours of sunlight an area on earth receives on any given day is determined by the tilt of the earth and its position in its orbit around the sun. The earth is tilted on its axis at 23 1/2°. This means that the rays of sunlight reach some areas of earth more directly than others at different times of the year. At some point during the year, the sun's rays will shine directly on the earth in the area from 23 1/2° north latitude, which is called the **Tropic of Cancer** to 23 1/2° south latitude, which is called the **Tropic of Capricorn**. As you get farther north or south of the equator, the angle at which the sun's rays strike the earth increases. This means the sunlight is less intense there. As the earth moves around the sun in its orbit, the part of the earth that is pointed toward the sun changes. This means that the hours that sunlight is visible in any given location on earth changes. For example, on June 21, the first day of summer in the Northern Hemisphere, people living in the Northern Hemisphere have the most daylight hours in a day and the fewest nighttime hours. In fact, people living near the North Pole have 24 hours of daylight on this date. As the earth moves in its orbit and winter approaches, the Northern Hemisphere receives fewer hours of daylight each day, and the Southern Hemisphere receives more hours of daylight. On December 21, the Southern Hemisphere has its longest day and shortest night. In locations around the equator, there is always approximately 12 hours of daylight because the sun shines directly on these areas.

Day and Night on Earth: Word Search

Directions: Read the clues below and figure out what words the clues represent. Then find and circle the words in the word search puzzle. Words can go horizontally, vertically, and diagonally in all eight directions.

```
Z E T V D X D T E R M I N A T O R R P L R
N N N X Q P Q M Z G R R W X M D J B R T Z
T I R E C N A C F O C I P O R T T N J K N
J L S R T R Y N E Q U A T O R T M M Q H F
D E J O W G Q V H Z J K G L Q F P L K T M
L T T L U K Q F N R M S D F T V R N R R N
M A M N W T V Q W C G E H D R T I D B O N
F D K F F N H N N R T T H K I L M H H P B
Z L R D N R N P A Z Q A B B T J E B H I Y
V A B B V T K X O Z R T R N D T M H T C N
B N R Q L Q I X E L P O G R W M E D X O R
F O N Q J S X D Y L E R K H R R R C L F Q
V I V T N T Y X T B O P H Q N T I N R C Z
C T N K P N I L N X G P D K R Y D R G A K
T A V T N T R M B Y V L H W R L I F K P D
V N C Q Y H P L E N N O D T R P A C Z R D
K R C A Y L L P J Z U T Y W R L N N N I B
J E D Y H P P M J R O P W H M O K Q B C K
K T T F R E D U T I G N O L R T N X C O P
G N J J B J B F Z C W K E M G Y L N T R K
K I M K X G Y K H M B C G S N P B J M N J
```

1. imaginary line through the center of the earth _____
2. 24 hours _____
3. always has about 12 hours of daylight each day _____
4. The earth moves 15 degrees of longitude every _____.
5. 180° longitude (three words) _____
6. Earth is divided into 360 degrees of this _____
7. has 24 hours of daylight on June 21 (two words) _____
8. path around the sun _____
9. 0° longitude (two words) _____
10. spins _____
11. has 24 hours of darkness on June 21 (two words) _____
12. line dividing daylight and darkness _____
13. keep track of local time (two words) _____
14. 23 1/2°N latitude (three words) _____
15. 23 1/2°S latitude (three words) _____

Earth's Wind Belts

The winds on Earth generally tend to blow from a certain direction at different latitudes. On any given day, the wind may blow from any direction, but there are general trends as to which direction the winds blow and, therefore, which direction weather moves. These general wind patterns are called **prevailing winds**.

There are three major **wind belts** north and south of the equator. Winds blow because there is a difference in the pressure of different air masses. Warm air near the equator moves toward the colder poles. Cold air near the poles moves toward the equator. However, the winds in each wind belt do not blow directly north and south. Because the earth has a spherical shape, it rotates fastest at the equator. This difference in the rotating speed causes the winds to be deflected either right or left in each wind belt. This phenomenon is called the **Coriolis Effect**.

The **trade wind belts** are located between the equator and 30° north and south latitude. The **northeast trade winds** blow from the northeast toward the southwest. The **southeast trade winds** blow from the southeast toward the northwest. Weather that begins in the Atlantic is blown west by the trade winds. This often brings hurricanes and tropical storms from the Atlantic to the Caribbean, Gulf Coast, or Atlantic Coast of the United States.

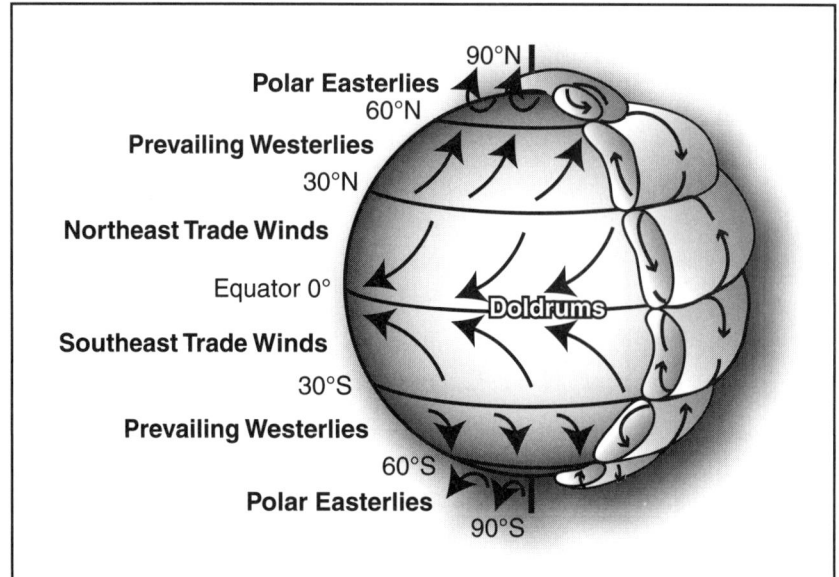

In the Northern Hemisphere, the **prevailing westerlies wind belt** is between 30°N and 60°N. Winds blow from the southwest to the northeast. The prevailing westerlies in the Southern Hemisphere are located from 30°S to 60°N, and the winds blow from the northwest to the southeast. In this belt, weather usually forms in the west and is blown toward the east.

The **polar easterlies wind belts** are from 60° to 90° north and south. In the Northern Hemisphere, the polar easterlies blow from northeast to southwest. In the Southern Hemisphere, the polar easterlies blow from southeast to northwest.

Near the equator, there is a region known as the **doldrums**. In this area, the air is settling down to the earth's surface. Therefore, on most days in the doldrums, there is very little wind. What wind does blow may be from any direction. In the days of sailing ships, captains tried to steer clear of the doldrums because there might not be enough wind to move a ship for days.

Two other regions of calm winds are at 30°N and 30°S. Many times, ships were caught in the region for so long with no wind to move them that the sailors ran short of water. They would have to throw the horses overboard to save water for themselves, so these regions became known as the **horse latitudes**.

World Geography Puzzles   Earth's Wind Belts

Name: _____ Date: _____

Earth's Wind Belts: Crossword Puzzle

Directions: Use the clues below to complete the crossword puzzle. All the words are related to Earth's wind belts.

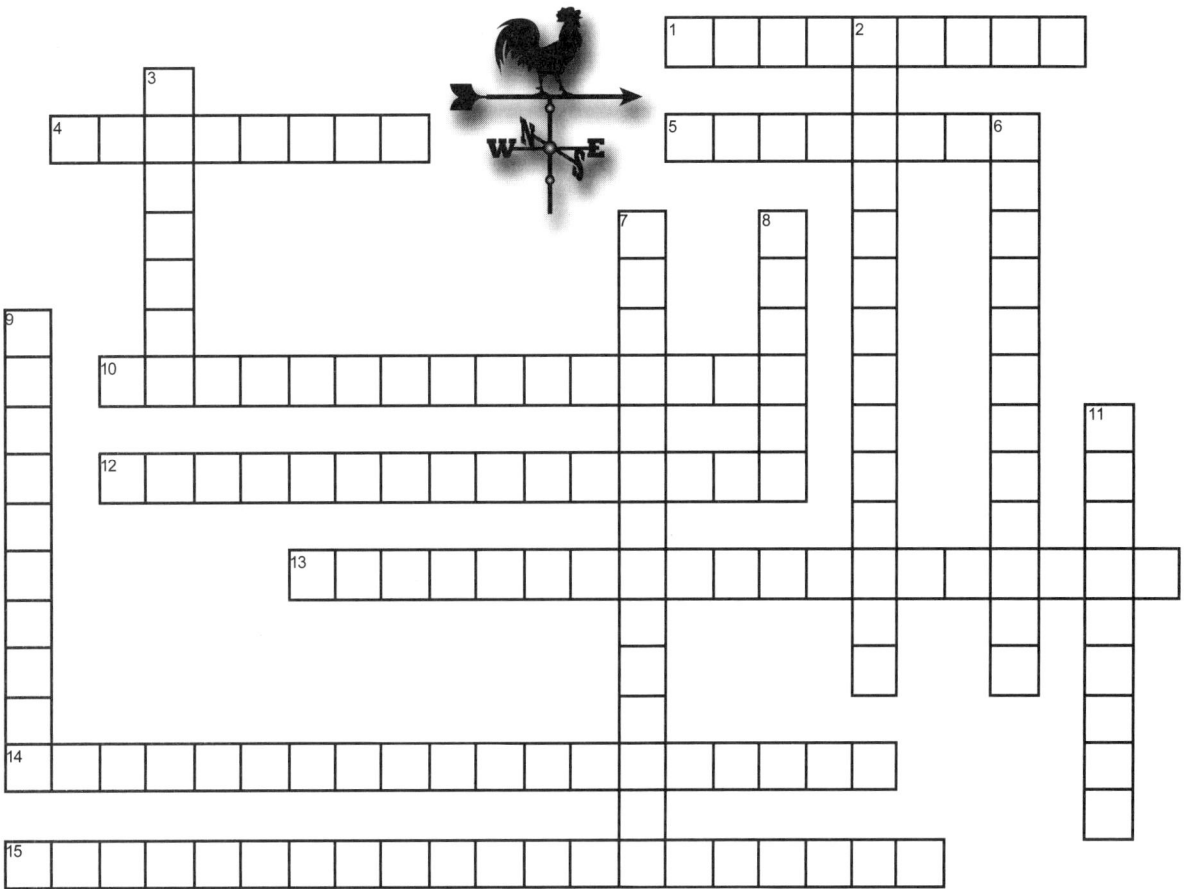

ACROSS

1. In the Southern Hemisphere, the polar easterlies blow from the _____ to the northwest.
4. Winds blow because there is a difference in the _____ of different air masses.
5. Area near the equator where air settles down to the earth's surface and there is little wind
10. General trends as to which direction winds blow from at certain latitudes (two words)
12. Wind belt located at 60° to 90° north and south latitudes (two words)
13. 0° to 30°N—blow from the northeast toward the southwest (three words)
14. 0° to 30°S—blow from the southeast toward the northwest (three words)
15. Wind belt located at 30° to 60° north and south latitudes (two words)

DOWN

2. Regions of calm winds at 30°N and 30°S (two words)
3. In the United States, _____ usually forms in the west and is blown east by the prevailing westerlies.
6. Captains of _____ _____ tried to steer clear of the doldrums.
7. Difference in rotating speeds causes winds to be deflected right or left in each wind belt. (two words)
8. When they ran short of water after being caught with no wind, sailors threw these overboard.
9. In the Atlantic Ocean, _____ are blown west by the trade winds.
11. There are three major _____ _____ north and south of the equator.

CD-404133 © Mark Twain Media, Inc., Publishers

Ocean Currents

The water in the oceans moves in currents. The **currents** are flowing streams of water that move through the oceans like great rivers. The currents generally move in a circular pattern. They move along the equator, then north along a coast, then across the open ocean again, and then south along another coast, back to the equator. This pattern is reversed in the Southern Hemisphere.

Currents may be either warm or cold. A **warm current** is when the flowing current is warmer than the surrounding water. It is flowing away from the equator. A **cold current** is when the flowing current is colder than the surrounding water. It is flowing toward the equator.

One example of a circular pattern of ocean currents is in the North Atlantic. The **North Equatorial Current** is a warm current moving west along the equator. This current then turns north and flows along the east coast of the United States. It then becomes the **Gulf Stream Current**, which is still a warm current. This brings warm water to an area off the coast of Newfoundland. This is a rich fishing area called the **Grand Banks**. The current then continues as the **North Atlantic Drift**, which flows northeast across the Atlantic toward Ireland. It is still a warm current that brings much warmer water to the British Isles than would be expected for the latitude. As the current turns southward and flows along the coasts of Europe and Africa, it is colder than the surrounding water, so it is a cold current. It is now called the **Canary Current**. This flows south until it reaches the equator and again becomes the North Equatorial Current.

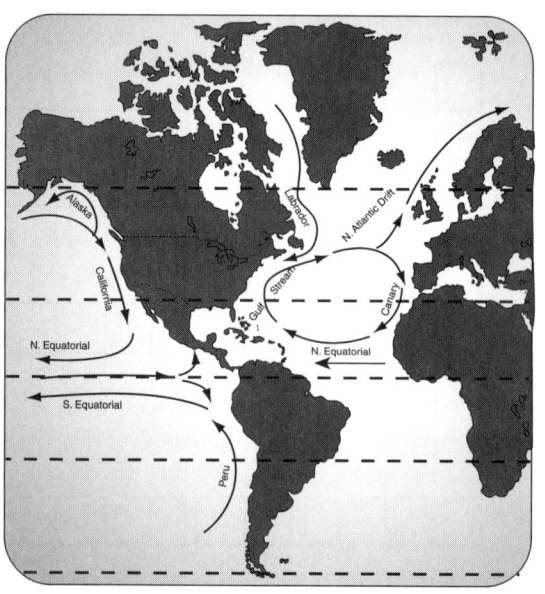

Ocean currents can affect the climates of the land areas near where they flow. For example, winds blowing over the warm North Atlantic Drift bring warm air to the British Isles. Because of this, the weather there is much milder than would be expected at that latitude. The air masses also pick up a lot of water vapor from the current, so there is foggy, drizzly, and cloudy weather in Ireland and Great Britain. The cold **California Current** flows from north to south along the west coast of the United States. The cold current cools the air over it, and the air masses that blow over the current cannot hold much water vapor. When the cool winds come onshore, they contain little water vapor. Few clouds form, and there is little, if any, rainfall. Much of the California coast has a climate that is cool, dry, and sunny.

The warm **El Niño Current** is an example of how ocean currents can affect people around the world. Sometimes, unusually warm waters flow toward the coast of Peru, replacing the usually cold **Peru Current**. Because the cold water is no longer coming to the surface and bringing nutrients for fish to eat, the populations of fish off the coasts of Peru and Ecuador decrease. This causes a large decrease in the amount of fish that fishermen are able to catch. The warm waters also cause many changes in weather patterns in South America, North America, and around the world. Places that are usually dry may get lots of rain. Regions that usually have severe winters may have very mild weather. The changes are felt many miles away from the current.

Ocean Currents: Hidden Message

Directions: Use the clues below to find the words associated with ocean currents. Write the words on the blanks provided. Then unscramble the circled letters to find a hidden message.

1. Flowing streams of water that move through the oceans like rivers _ _ _ _ _ _ _ _

2. Rich fishing area off the coast of Newfoundland _ _ _ _ _ _ _ _ _ _

3. Name of the cold curent that flows from north to south along the west coast of the United States _ _ _ _ _ _ _ _ _

4. Warm current that moves west along the equator in the North Atlantic _ _ _ _ _ _ _ _ _ _ _ _ _

5. Cold current that moves from south to north along the coasts of Chile, Peru, and Ecuador _ _ _ _

6. Warm air masses pick up a lot of this in the North Atlantic and create foggy, drizzly weather in Ireland and Great Britain. _ _ _ _ _ _ _ _ _ _

7. Cold current that flows southward along the coasts of Europe and Africa _ _ _ _ _ _

8. When the flowing current is warmer than the surrounding water _ _ _ _ _ _ _ _ _

9. Warm current that flows northward along the east coast of the United States _ _ _ _ _ _ _ _ _

10. When the flowing current is colder than the surrounding water _ _ _ _ _ _ _ _ _ _

11. Currents generally move in this type of pattern. _ _ _ _ _ _ _

12. Warm current that flows northeast across the Atlantic toward Ireland _ _ _ _ _ _ _ _ _ _ _ _ _ _ _ _ _

Unscramble the circled letters to find this unusually warm current that is an example of how ocean currents can affect people around the world.

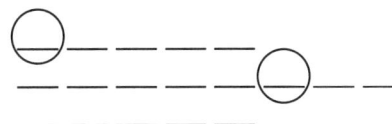

Cultures From Around the World

When you study how people live, you are studying their **culture**. In every country and community, you will find that people behave in unique ways. The language people speak, the special foods they eat, and the clothes they wear are all a part of their culture. In other words, you are studying everything about their way of life.

You will find that the foods eaten and the clothes worn are often different in other parts of the world than what you are used to. There are certain foods that are prepared for special occasions. Many times, people wear specific kinds of clothes for these occasions. For special days like weddings, there are traditional ways of doing things.

There are many customs and traditions practiced in the United States that are found in other places around the world, as well. This is because many citizens of the United States have come from other cultures to live in this country. When people come to the United States from another country, they are called **immigrants**. These immigrants bring their customs and traditions with them; these then become part of the way of life in the United States. Many of the traditions and customs in our homes were brought to our country many years ago by family members who immigrated from another country. When we go in to a new community, we may find customs and traditions different from those we have known. This is what makes the United States a country of many cultures.

People from other cultures have also added words from their languages to the English we speak today in the United States. For example, *zucchini* is from Italian, *patio* is from Spanish, *kindergarten* is from German, *tundra* is from Russian, *waffle* is from Dutch, *jubilee* is from Hebrew, *ketchup* is from Chinese, and *chipmunk* is from a Native American language.

The holidays we celebrate and the foods we eat on those special days are customs or traditions. Many of us have turkey on Thanksgiving Day. Often, there is a special food for Easter. Palm Sunday is a special day in Peru. It is a religious holiday with music, food, and dancing. The customary foods for this day are cabrito, yucca, and sweet potatoes. St. Patrick's Day was brought to the United States by the Irish. St. Patrick is recognized as the patron saint of Ireland. St. Patrick's Day is still celebrated as a religious holiday in Ireland, but in the United States, it has become a full-blown secular celebration with parades, green decorations, shamrocks, and foods such as corned beef and cabbage.

For some occasions, there are certain clothes to wear. In some communities, the clothes are brightly colored. In other communities, people wear very plain clothing. There may be a requirement for women or men to wear special head or face coverings.

All of these food, clothing, language, and ceremonial customs are part of a group's culture and they make that group unique. Each group of people can learn new things from others. This helps us become aware of new ways of doing things and helps us appreciate the strengths and weaknesses of each culture.

World Geography Puzzles | Cultures From Around the World

Name: _____ Date: _____

Cultures From Around the World: Word Scramble

Directions: Use the clues below to unscramble the words that are associated with cultures from around the world. Write the words on the lines provided.

1. People who come to the United States from another country — NIRSMIGTMA _____

2. How people live; their way of life — CEUUTRL _____

3. The words, pronunciations, and grammar used and understood by a community as a means of communication — UNGGAEAL _____

4. Holiday or special occasion — COLNBIREAET _____

5. Special traditions, foods, or clothing of a group — CMSTUSO _____

6. Some communities may require women or men to wear head or face _____. — VEOINSRCG _____

7. Kindergarten is from this language. — ERGAMN _____

8. St. Patrick's Day is mainly a religious holiday in _____. — LDNEARI _____

9. One of the customary foods for Palm Sunday in Peru — WTEES TETASOOP _____

10. Chipmunk is a word from a _____ _____ language. — EAINVT CEAMRIAN _____

11. A day when many Americans eat turkey — GINSKNAHVTGI _____

12. Brightly colored _____ are a tradition in some communities. — TEOLCSH _____

13. Ketchup is from this language. — IESHNCE _____

14. People with common interests and customs living in a particular area — NIMUCTOYM _____

15. A special day where there are traditional ways of doing things, such as specific kinds of clothes, ceremonies, and foods — EWDGNID _____

CD-404133 © Mark Twain Media, Inc., Publishers

Location

Location is one of the five themes of geography. It examines the position of people and places on the surface of the earth. Location can be expressed in absolute or relative terms.

Absolute location is a street address or the latitude and longitude grid coordinates for a place on Earth. A certain business is located at 1125 Washington Street, or Denver, Colorado, is located at 40°N, 105°W.

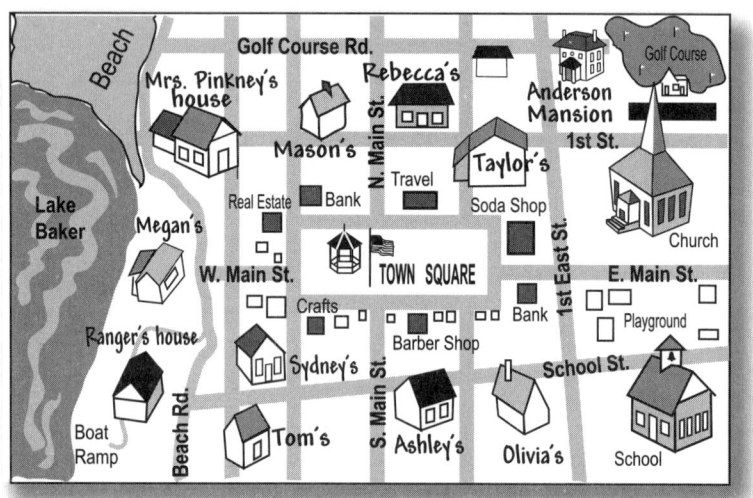
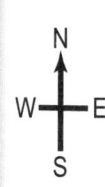

Relative location describes where a place can be found in terms of other places and how they relate to each other. The Rocky Mountains are located between the Great Plains and Intermontane plateaus and basins of the American West; Utah is located north of Arizona. Where a place is located is important relative to other places and in how we perceive and are influenced by that location.

In order to find the absolute location of a city, country, river, mountain, or desert, you can use an atlas. An **atlas** is a book of maps. Usually, an atlas includes maps of all the continents on Earth. An atlas includes an **index** where all the named locations are listed alphabetically. To find the location of a place you are looking for, turn to the index and find the place name in the list. The index lists the page number of the map where you can find the place you are looking for. It also lists the latitude and longitude coordinates. Use the coordinates by first finding the line of latitude or estimating where that line would be on the map. Then follow that line to the left or right until you intersect the line of longitude you are looking for. Somewhere near this point should be the location you are seeking.

For example, if you are trying to find Tokyo, Japan, you would turn to the index and find this listing: Tokyo, Japan 147   36°N   140°E. This means that Tokyo is on a map on page 147. It can be found at 36° north latitude and 140° east longitude. This is the absolute location. Once you have found Tokyo on the map, you can see where it is in relation to other places. It is roughly in the middle of the island of Honshu on the east coast. It is next to a natural bay and is north of Yokohama.

When you know the location of a place, you can start to get an idea about what is important in that place. Since Tokyo is located on an island in the Pacific Ocean and it has a natural bay where ships could anchor safely, it is a good guess that fishing, shipping, and trade would be important parts of the economy. The location of a place helps determine what businesses prosper there, such as agriculture or manufacturing, how many people travel through the area, how they trade with the rest of the world, what type of government might work in the area, and even what type of clothes the people are likely to wear throughout the year.

World Geography Puzzles   Location

Name: _____ Date: _____

Location: Word Search

Directions: Find and circle the locations in the word search puzzle. Words can go horizontally, vertically, and diagonally in all eight directions. When you have found all the words in the puzzle, use an atlas or the Internet to find the latitude and longitude coordinates for each location and write them on the lines provided.

1. HONOLULU
   _____

2. MOUNT EVEREST
   _____

3. GLASGOW
   _____

4. KYOTO
   _____

5. LAKE MICHIGAN
   _____

6. SYDNEY
   _____

7. CAPE TOWN
   _____

8. SASKATOON
   _____

```
K E T N O Z I R O H O L E B C T T K
N W O T E P A C N H L V Q V L S O L
D G T K N Y C F R O L N C P E K P T
U X M M D T D N G P O I F R G F X K
B V E R A C R U Z D N T E N P P P K
L R I H F F Q Q L C K V A N V K M V
I K V X H F Z M I X E B K K L T K L
N D Y M A S L N X T K U G R S T G A
Y L L O Y P N G N W I L D L T A K K
Q R U D T A O U X A P U K V T Q S E
B A N X T O O T H N G L A S G O W M
R E R I E M D G O C J O R A Y R Q I
Y S Y V Z M N K X C J N Z T K X H C
K L W H M A B R M D T O R R R L N H
Z A Q K H R F O L C W H B A H T J I
M R G S R P Q Q U F D K X K K L G G
M A Q Q A Y E R S R O C K A L F G A
G D A R G O G L O V G M Z J X F R N
```

9. ARAL SEA
    _____

10. BANGKOK
    _____

11. VERACRUZ
    _____

12. LUXEMBOURG
    _____

13. DUBLIN
    _____

14. BELO HORIZONTE
    _____

15. CINCINNATI
    _____

16. COTOPAXI
    _____

17. VOLGOGRAD
    _____

18. JAKARTA
    _____

19. SHANGHAI
    _____

20. AYERS ROCK
    _____

Place

The theme of **place** describes those physical and human characteristics that make every location on the earth's surface unique. This includes the **physical characteristics** of a place, such as the geology and hydrology of a location, the climate, soil, and the types of plants and animals a place can support. These things are all part of the natural environment. **Human characteristics** of place include aspects of human culture, such as housing styles, communication and transportation networks, and systems of government, belief, and economic interaction. These are all the man-made features and customs of a place.

Both physical and human characteristics provide answers to the question, "What makes this place unique?" For example, when you think of Switzerland, you might think of snow-covered mountains, clear lakes, and grassy pastures with milk cows. You might also think of people who dress in brightly colored traditional costumes, mountain chalets made of wood and plaster, ski resorts, a government that remains neutral in wartime, and delicious chocolate. All of these things help to describe what Switzerland is and how it is different from any other place on Earth.

When you are describing a place, it helps if you can develop a personal connection with the place. What does the place mean to you? Even if you have never been to the place, you probably know something about the history, people, customs, climate, animals, or architecture of the area. Whether it is your favorite neighborhood park or a city halfway around the world, every place has its own story. If you can tell the story of the place, you can do a good job of describing it.

Travel and tourism agencies depend on the idea of place. Through advertising in magazines, on the radio and television, and on the Internet, they are trying to describe to people how unique their place is. They want people to be so interested that they decide to visit that place. From big cities to small towns, everyone wants people to visit their place, enjoy the sights and activities they have to offer, and spend money in the area while they are doing it. For example, Orlando, Florida, is known for huge theme parks; Kenya is known as a place to go on safari and see exotic animals; and Paris, France, is known a city of great art, architecture, and romance. However, there are also places known for having the largest ball of string, being the birthplace of bluegrass music, or being the hometown of a former president. All these places have physical and human characteristics that make them special.

World Geography Puzzles   Place

Name: _____ Date: _____

Place: Describe It

Directions: Look at the picture below. Write as many words as you can think of to describe this place. Think of the physical characteristics, such as the climate, the geology, and the vegetation. Also think of the human characteristics of this place, such as transportation, communication, and architecture. Use the words to make a puzzle or activity of your own.

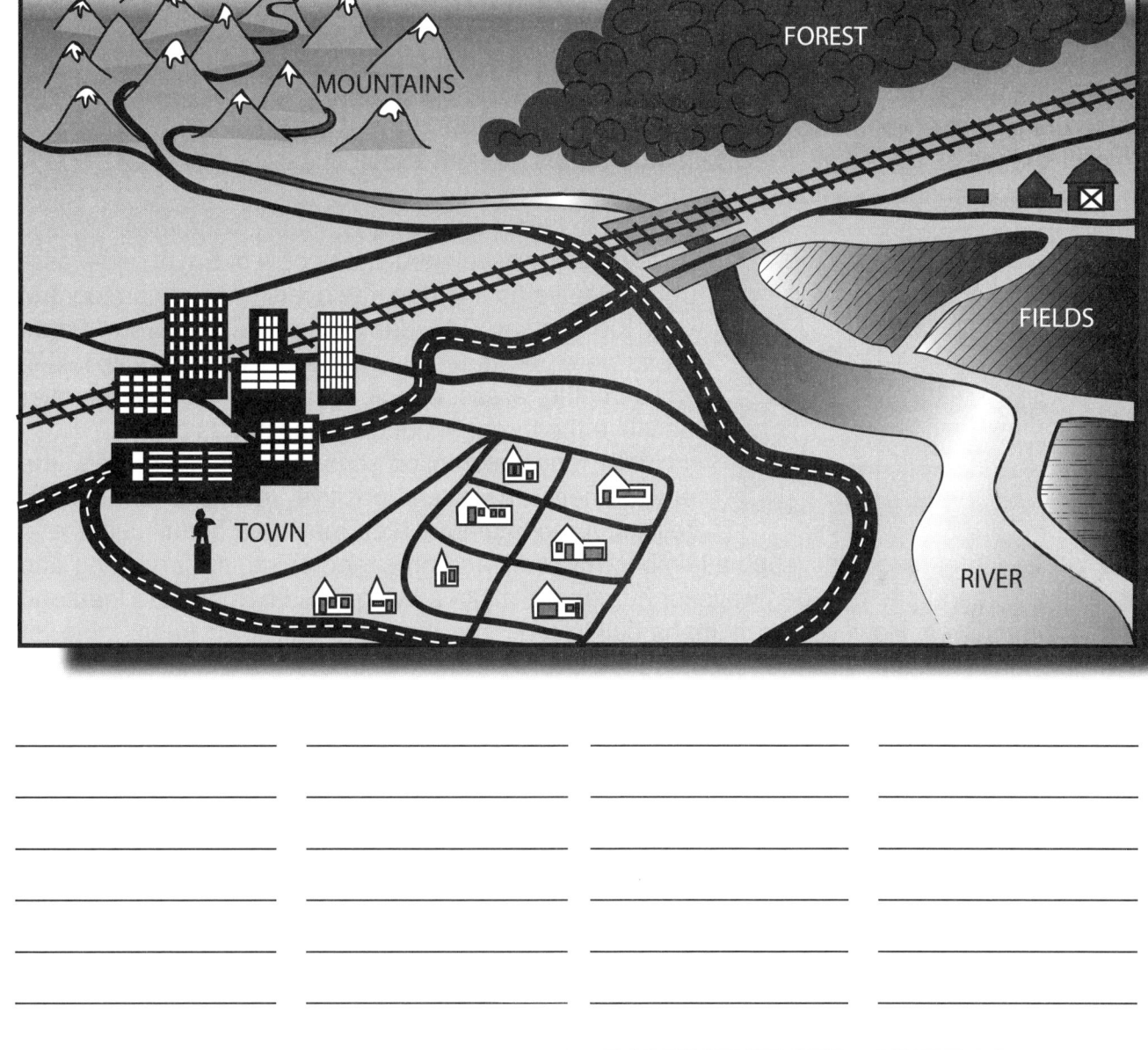

Human-Environment Interaction

One of the themes of geography is human-environment interaction. These are the cultural and physical relationships that result from people adjusting their lifestyle to the physical conditions that are unique to the place where they are living. It also traces ways people alter the world around them to better meet their survival needs. In other words, it is how the land affects people and how people affect the land.

The environment, or physical surroundings, is an important factor in the lifestyle of people. For example, in the river valleys of Egypt and Mesopotamia, the rivers would flood every year. This built up areas of fertile soil near the rivers. People soon learned how to plant and grow crops in these areas. While the flooding could bring destruction, it also allowed the people to grow plenty of food for themselves and to trade with others. This brought about the first stable economies and governments in history.

People can also have an impact on the environment. As technology developed, the people of Egypt and Mesopotamia were able to dam the rivers to gain more control over the flooding. The dams changed the rivers. Some areas were permanently flooded and covered with lakes, while in other areas, people could live closer to the river because the threat of flooding was not as great.

With any interaction between humans and the environment, there are positive results and negative results. A mountainous area may be a beautiful place to live that is rich in resources, such as timber, minerals and ores, and animals. Harvesting and using these resources provides ways for humans to make a living, build homes, and feed and clothe themselves. However, as humans build roads into the area, cut down trees, mine for minerals, and hunt animals, the resources are depleted and the landscape is changed. It may become a place where no one wants to live anymore.

Why do some places become large metropolitan areas, while others remain rural and agricultural? Why do more older, retired people live in a certain area and lots of young families live in another area? The soil types and landforms, climate, and access to transportation routes play a big role in shaping how the people live.

Human-Environment Interaction: Crossword Puzzle

Directions: Use the clues below to find ways that humans interact with their environment. Then write the words in the crossword puzzle.

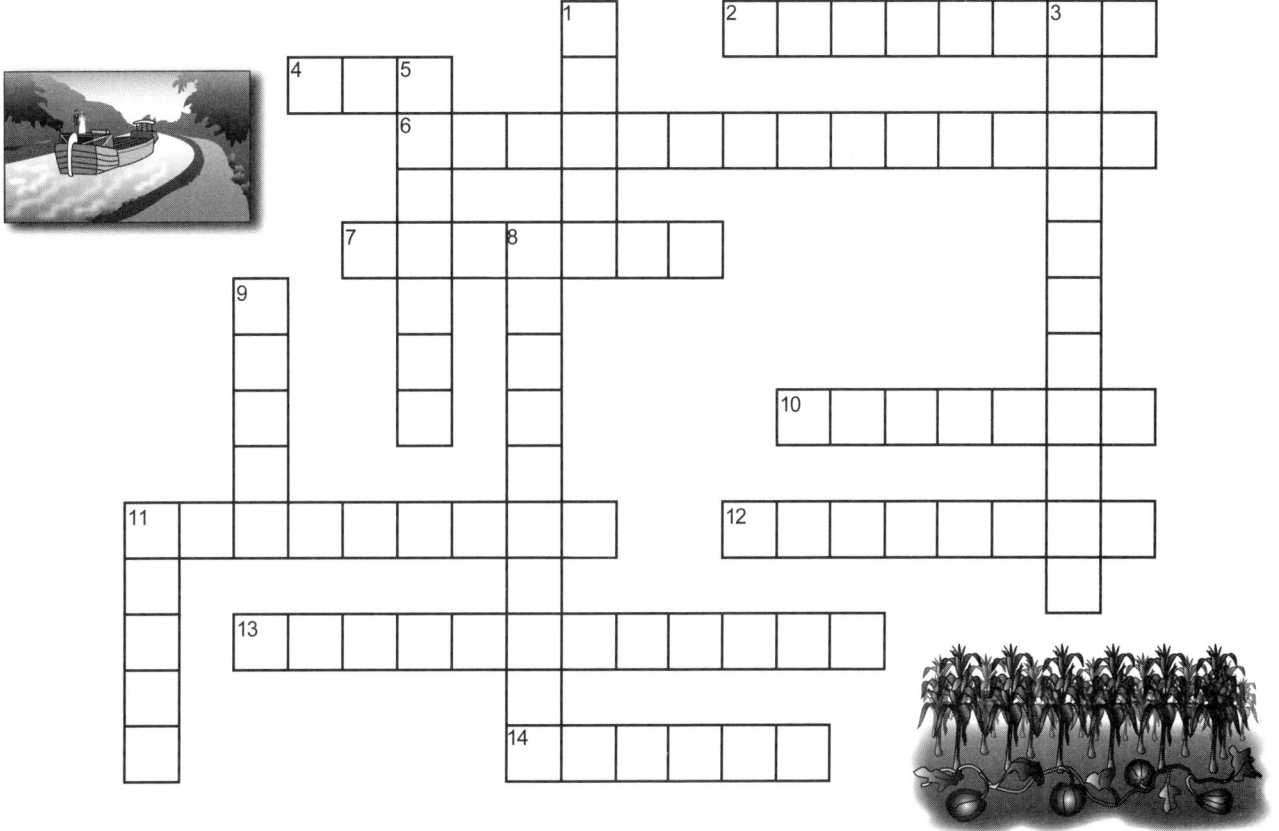

ACROSS
2. Tracks built so trains can haul people and freight from place to place
4. A structure built across a river to hold back water
6. The basic framework of roads, electric lines, water and gas pipes, fiber optic cables, etc.
7. To make land suitable for commercial or residential purposes, such as building stores or houses for rent or sale
10. To contaminate the environment with man-made waste
11. To remove all the trees in a stand of timber (hyphenated word)
12. Managing forests and growing timber
13. The process of turning into a city
14. Extracting minerals from the ground

DOWN
1. Relating to agricultural or sparsely populated areas; the country
3. Cultivating the land, producing crops, and raising livestock
5. A naturally occurring substance usually obtained from the ground, such as coal, iron ore, or petroleum
8. Visiting a location to enjoy the unique plants and animals of that region
9. An embankment built along the side of a river to control flooding
11. A man-made waterway for navigation, drainage, or irrigation

Movement

Movement is the geographic theme that describes the ways and reasons people, products, and ideas move about the surface of the earth. It involves both communication and transportation of materials and ideas. Transporting raw materials to a factory, distributing products to consumers, the distances consumers will travel to purchase from a particular location, and the methods used to communicate advertisements and ideas over time and space are all examples of movement.

What kinds of things move in our society? First of all, people move. People may move into an area because it has fertile land for growing crops or because there is an industry in the area offering jobs. They may move to the area because the climate is better for their health or just more comfortable for them. People may leave an area when an industry shuts down, when the environment becomes polluted, when a natural or manmade disaster strikes the area, or when crime increases in the area.

Raw materials and products move into and out of areas all the time. If the land is used for agriculture, equipment, seeds, fertilizers, and other chemicals are brought into the area to

farm the land and produce crops. When the crops, such as corn, soybeans, cotton, or wheat, are harvested, they are then moved out of the area to be processed into food, clothing, or other products. If an area has manufacturing plants, the materials to build the plants and the equipment in the plants need to be brought in. Raw materials, such as iron ore, coal, lumber, cotton, chemicals, or other items, are needed to manufacture the finished goods. Then, the manufactured goods, such as cars, textiles, furniture, computers, shampoo, or books, are sent out to be sold.

Ideas are another thing that move. Religions, systems of government, languages, educational ideas, and entertainment are all examples of intangible thoughts and ideas that move around the world. In the past, these ideas came with the people as they moved into an area. This may have been a gradual change and blending of ideas over decades, or there may have been a sudden influx of new people in only a few years. Today, thanks to the Internet and news and entertainment media, there doesn't have to be a great movement of people for ideas to move around the globe. People can watch television, listen to the radio, and search the world wide web to find information on every topic known to man.

As new technology develops, the methods and reasons for movement change. Movement of people, goods, and ideas is different today than it was in the past, and it will continue to change in the future. People used to have to move themselves and their goods by walking, floating down a river, or using animals to pull carts and wagons. There are some places in the world where this is still the only way to get from place to place. However, as technology advanced, railroads and locomotives were built to move large amounts of goods and people over long distances. Eventually, automobiles, such as cars, trucks, and tractor trailers, on highways made transportation to almost any place easier and cost-effective. Now airplanes fly to almost every place on Earth. These routes and systems of transportation including railroads, rivers, highways, airports, fiber-optic networks, and satellite systems, are called **infrastructure**.

World Geography Puzzles　　　　　　　　　　　　　　　　Movement

Name: _____ Date: _____

Movement: Decoding

Directions: Decode the missing words in the text below by using the code key at the bottom of the page.

1. __ __ __ __ __ __ move because of availability of jobs, to take advantage of climate,
   4 21 10 4 6 21
   or to avoid a disaster or polluted area.

2. __ __ __ __ __ __ __ __ describes the ways and reasons people, products, and
   20 10 11 21 20 21 16 3
   ideas move about the surface of the earth.

3. Movement involves both __ __ __ __ __ __ __ __ __ __ __ __ __ and
   2 10 20 20 17 16 25 2 8 3 25 10 16
   transportation of materials and ideas.

4. Equipment, seeds, and fertilizer are brought in, while crops are moved out of an area
   involved in __ __ __ __ __ __ __ __ __ __ __.
   8 1 26 25 2 17 6 3 17 26 21

5. In a __ __ __ __ __ __ __ __ __ __ __ __ plant, raw materials are brought in
   20 8 16 17 9 8 2 3 17 26 25 16 1
   and finished goods are shipped out.

6. Ideas, such as religion, systems of government, __ __ __ __ __ __ __ __ __,
   6 8 16 1 17 8 1 21 19
   education, and entertainment, move around the world as people travel or communicate.

7. What used to take decades to travel from one country to another can now be transmitted
   almost instantly on the __ __ __ __ __ __ __ __ __ __ __.
   23 10 26 6 15   23 25 15 21 23 21 18

8. __ __ __ __ __ __ __ __ __ __ __, such as iron ore, lumber, or cotton, are
   26 8 23 20 8 3 21 26 25 8 6 19
   used to manufacture finished goods.

9. The routes and systems of transportation that include highways, railroads, and satellite
   systems, are called __ __ __ __ __ __ __ __ __ __ __ __ __.
   25 16 9 26 8 19 3 26 17 2 3 17 26 21

10. One of the earliest modes of transportation was floating down a __ __ __ __ __, but
    26 25 11 21 26
    today, people can fly on an airplane to almost any place on Earth.

A	B	C	D	E	F	G	H	I	J	K	L	M	N	O	P	Q	R	S	T	U	V	W	X	Y	Z
8	18	2	15	21	9	1	7	25	22	14	6	20	16	10	4	24	26	19	3	17	11	23	12	5	13

Regions

The **regions** theme of geography looks at the common physical and human characteristics that link a place to other parts of the world. It explores how groups of people, the production of specific products, and the spread of specific ideas are linked together. Regions range from physical places to language groups to zones of development and decay in a city.

There are many characteristics used to describe regions. The world can be divided into regions by political boundaries or by geographical features. The continent of Africa is a geographical region. The Alps, the Himalyas, and the Rockies are part of the mountain regions of the world. The European Union is a political region consisting of European countries that have entered into cooperative agreements. Language can be a characteristic used to describe a region. The Slavic speaking countries of eastern Europe are a region. Regions can also be defined by what goods are produced in the area. There are mining regions, agricultural regions, oil-producing regions, manufacturing regions, and fishing regions. Within each region may be more specific regions, such as the Corn Belt or the diamond mining region.

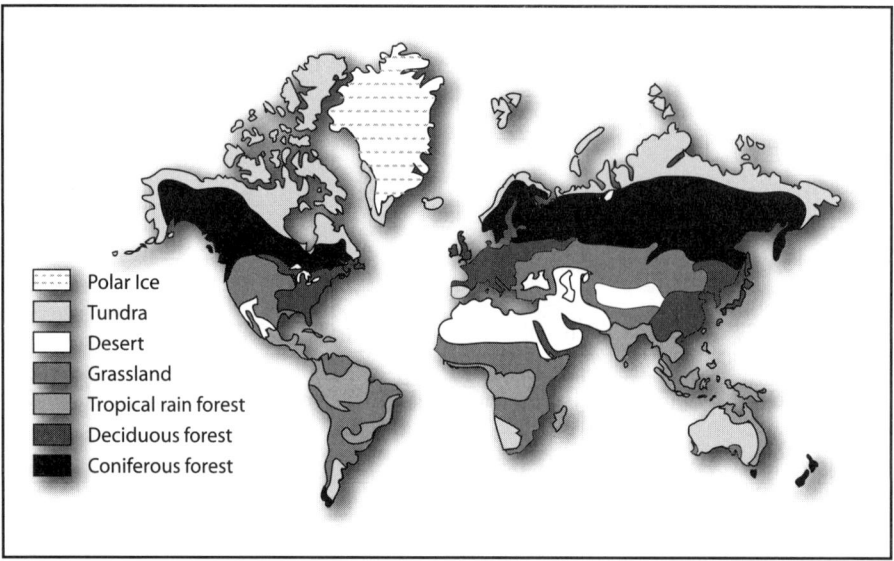

Places around the world that share the same climate can be grouped together in regions. There are deserts, rain forests, tundras, evergreen forests, and grasslands in many places on Earth. While each is unique, they all share similar traits that identify them as that kind of region.

Culture and religion can link people together in regions. For example, a map can show the different areas of the world where Christianity, Islam, or Judaism is the dominant religion. These are religious regions. There are regions where more people are likely to be nomads, moving from place to place to graze animals or for seasonal work. There are other regions where people are more likely to be involved in finance, computers, or entertainment and tourism. Food is a big part of the culture that can link people in different areas. Sometimes this is referred to as regional cuisine or regional food. Such things as Mexican food, Thai food, Italian food, Chinese food, and many others represent the type of food eaten in regions around the world.

As with all the themes, the concept of a region helps us organize the world so we can understand it better. Regions help us deal with bite-sized pieces of the world, instead of the whole thing at once. For example, we can just discuss French-speaking countries, see how the countries in that region are alike and different, and see how they relate to the rest of the world.

Regions: Word Search

Directions: Find and circle the words listed below in the word search puzzle. Words can go horizontally, vertically, and diagonally in all eight directions. All of the words represent a region or regions on Earth.

```
K T W N T J A C I R E M A L A R T N E C P M
Y R M H K G O C E A N I A K Y C R N G B R Y
A N D E S M O U N T A I N S K V N S R E C N
M M K D D T K N B P W T W P N R G O A N C N
V C L J R I A I S E N Y L O P B D U S E V I
V F W R F K T J C T R O P I C A L T S L A S
K T Z W V T L E F F Y M S M O D V H L U N A
T P H A G I A T R T M A Z U L T J E A X N B
R G C E N N M C R R Y T T L E T R A N C A O
O V R M M B I E N A A B R M Q E R S D O V G
C C B E G I S S L N A N P Y G C C T W U A N
K H N C A E D A A C S E E A T A T A L N S O
Y A P R D T M D K B R N U A N B E S P T K C
M I J A H I P R L A N G A D N N B I R R H S
O N T L H B H L T E N O I K I Z R A N I T L
U O K O N H K E A A E N Z P L D G U H E C A
N G X P B A F F L I A A L A W A Q N R S L V
T A X C Q O R U T V N A S M M Q B N P A V I
A T M X R R T D I F Y S D T F A Z L K W L C
I A C E Y N D A N W Z R P M Y C M K N L N Y
N P S Z A V W Y L U K J M J X W R Q R Q R F
S T C B X U R B A N T C T N G N B M Q J N X
```

ALPINE
AMAZON BASIN
ANDES MOUNTAINS
BALKANS
BANTU LANGUAGE
BENELUX COUNTRIES
CENTRAL AMERICA
CONGO BASIN
DESERT
GRASSLAND

GREAT PLAINS
HIMALAYAS
MEDITERRANEAN
OCEANIA
OUTBACK
PATAGONIA
POLAR
POLYNESIA
ROCKY MOUNTAINS
RURAL

SAVANNA
SCANDINAVIA
SLAVIC
SOUTHEAST ASIA
TAIGA
TEMPERATE FOREST
THE MIDDLE EAST
TROPICAL
TUNDRA
URBAN

North America: Locations of Major Cities

Directions: Location is the position of a place on Earth's surface. The absolute location is the latitude and longitude coordinates of a place. Using an atlas or the Internet, find the absolute locations below and fill in the name of the city at that location in the crossword puzzle. Coordinates may vary slightly from atlas to atlas.

ACROSS

1. 42°N, 88°W
4. 9°N, 80°W
6. 34°N, 118°W
9. 39°N, 105°W
12. 30°N, 90°W
14. 19°N, 99°W
16. 10°N, 84°W
17. 26°N, 80°W
18. 13°N, 89°W
19. 41°N, 74°W

DOWN

2. 61°N, 149°W
3. 45°N, 76°W
5. 26°N, 100°W
7. 62°N, 114°W
8. 49°N, 123°W
10. 38°N, 77°W
11. 15°N, 91°W
13. 48°N, 53°W
14. 12°N, 86°W
15. 17°N, 88°W

World Geography Puzzles North America

Name: _____ Date: _____

North America: Physical Features

Directions: Find and circle the name of each physical geographical feature in the word search puzzle. Below each feature, write the state, province, or country where it is located.

```
T Y R Z Q R D L Z G X H W C K T N C K L R
B H U D S O N B A Y F W H K K K F G M J G
T L M P Y N N R H L B M F R N N P L O H E
R E P I F J R C H B T Q C Y W L H L U X P
V K Y W S Q A R Q R C L R Q X T M C N M I
V A P B R S Z U L Y L R S L P B A Y T R N
L L L H A Y I K G N R E K O Q N C N M C N
M T M A N F B S Y A D N P Z A B O R C L I
L L B W N J F N S A R O R D H Y T T K T W
J A K W N A C I L I C A I Q N Y P L I T E
C S L B C P C G N A P A C A M M J K N W K
K T F R T R R A T I N P C I M P F Q L N A
Q A R Z Z E X E M S S D I G N L Z R E P L
R E G D V M P N H A N L X R N E Z Y Y C T
Y R Q E J E B I K A N B A H I M K N Z W D
L G E W T Y E F R L M A T N R V L A M R Z
T H X L L L T G B M L M P N D M E P L N C
T T W X D W R K X C K P K M Y H Y R L N J
L A T N E D I C C O E R D A M A R R E I S
X Y B L U E R I D G E M O U N T A I N S G
W G T R K G U L F O F C A L I F O R N I A
```

1. GREAT SALT LAKE
   _____

2. SIERRA MADRE OCCIDENTAL
   _____

3. THE EVERGLADES
   _____

4. HUDSON BAY
   _____

5. MISSISSIPPI RIVER
   _____

6. MOUNT McKINLEY
   _____

7. POPOCATEPETL
   _____

8. PANAMA CANAL
   _____

9. LAKE WINNIPEG
   _____

10. BLUE RIDGE MOUNTAINS
    _____

11. CANADIAN SHIELD
    _____

12. LAKE NICARAGUA
    _____

13. GULF OF CALIFORNIA
    _____

14. GRAND CANYON
    _____

15. BAFFIN ISLAND
    _____

CD-404133 © Mark Twain Media, Inc., Publishers

World Geography Puzzles   North America

Name: _____ Date: _____

North America: Plants, Animals, and Resources

Directions: Decode the missing words in the text below by using the code key at the bottom of the page.

    North America has a wide variety of plants and animals, industries, and valuable natural resources. Large deposits of __ __ __ __ __ __ __ __ __ (21 10 13 17 23 24 10 11 26) and natural gas are in Alaska, western Canada, the southwestern United States, and eastern Mexico. North America also has large deposits of __ __ __ __ (6 23 2 24) and iron ore. Gold and __ __ __ __ __ __ (15 18 24 9 10 17) are mined throughout the continent. __ __ __ __ __ __ __ __ __ __ (2 14 17 18 6 11 24 13 11 17 10) is a major industry throughout the continent. Grains and livestock are raised in the plains regions, while __ __ __ __ __ __ __ __ __ __ (6 2 24 18 12 23 17 25 18 2), Florida, and Texas produce fruits and __ __ __ __ __ __ __ __ __ (9 10 14 10 13 2 4 24 10 15). Forestry is a major industry in __ __ __ __ __ __ (6 2 25 2 8 2) and the western United States. __ __ __ __ __ __ __ (12 18 15 16 18 25 14) is the most important industry in Greenland and is done along the entire coast of the continent.

    Major __ __ __ __ __ __ (10 5 21 23 17 13 15) of the continent include food, chemicals, __ __ __ __ __ __ __ __ __ __ __ (26 2 6 16 18 25 10 17 3), forest products, metals, and __ __ __ __ __ __ (6 17 11 8 10) oil. Mexico and the Central American countries also export __ __ __ __ __ __ (6 23 12 12 10 10) and minerals.

    In addition to domesticated animals, the plains and prairies are home to mammals, such as __ __ __ __ __ __ __ __ (2 25 13 10 24 23 21 10), deer, __ __ __ __ __ __ __ (14 23 21 16 10 17 15), and prairie dogs. Larger mammals include __ __ __ __ __ __ (4 18 15 23 25), __ __ __ __ __ __ __ __ (6 2 17 18 4 23 11), moose, __ __ __ __ __ __ (20 2 14 11 2 17), oxen, and puma. The world's largest bears, the __ __ __ __ __ __ __ (14 17 18 1 1 24 3) bear and __ __ __ __ __ __ (21 23 24 2 17) bear, are found in North America. __ __ __ __ __ __ (7 16 2 24 10 15) and dolphins live in the waters off the coast of the continent.

    Reptiles in North America include poisonous snakes, such as the __ __ __ __ __ __ - __ __ __ __ (6 23 13 13 23 25 - 26 23 11 13 16), rattlesnake, and __ __ __ __ __ __ __ __ __ (6 23 21 21 10 17 16 10 2 8). The __ __ __ __ __ __ (4 10 2 8 10 8) lizard, the world's only poisonous lizard, lives in Mexico and the southwestern United States.

    North America's lakes and rivers are home to many species of __ __ __ __ __ - __ __ __ __ (12 17 10 15 16 - 7 2 13 10 17) fish. Many kinds of shellfish, __ __ __ __ __ __ __ (12 18 25 12 18 15 16), and __ __ __ __ __ __ (15 16 2 17 22 15), live in the coastal waters.

    More than 800 species of birds also inhabit the continent. They range from the tiny __ __ __ __ __ __ __ __ __ (16 11 26 26 18 25 14 4 18 17 8) to the large California __ __ __ __ __ __ (6 23 25 8 23 17). Marsh and inland water birds, such as __ __ __ __ __ __ __ (16 10 17 23 25 15), ducks, __ __ __ __ __ __ __ __ (21 10 24 18 6 2 25 15), and geese, are also plentiful. Central America is home to colorful __ __ __ __ __ __ __ (13 17 23 21 18 6 2 24) birds. Birds of __ __ __ __ (21 17 10 3) that live in North America include eagles, hawks, and __ __ __ __ __ __ __ (12 2 24 6 23 25 15).

A	B	C	D	E	F	G	H	I	J	K	L	M	N	O	P	Q	R	S	T	U	V	W	X	Y	Z
2	4	6	8	10	12	14	16	18	20	22	24	26	25	23	21	19	17	15	13	11	9	7	5	3	1

North America: Native Americans

Northwest totem pole

When the first Europeans came to North America, many tribes of people, who later became known as Indians, lived throughout the continent. Today, we generally refer to these people as **Native Americans**.

Anthropologists believe that these people were descended from the people of northeast Asia. It is commonly believed that, approximately 20,000 to 30,000 years ago, hunters looking for new hunting grounds crossed a **land bridge** that connected Asia and North America. The land bridge, which no longer exists, went across what is now the Bering Strait. These early hunters continued to move south into the rest of North America and eventually into Central and South America.

The Native American tribes are divided into several major cultural groups. The native inhabitants of the northern arctic and subarctic regions are also known as **Northern Hunters**. They included the Aleuts, Chipewyan, and Inuit (known as Eskimo). They are hunters of caribou, polar bear, walrus, and whale.

The **Woodland group** inhabited the eastern part of the continent. They grew crops and used wood for housing, weapons, utensils, and canoes. Major woodland tribes included the Algonquian-speaking tribes of Delaware, Chippewa, Massachusett, Micmac, and Pequot. The Iroquois-speaking woodland tribes included the Cayuga, Mohawk, Oneida, Onondaga, and Seneca.

The **Plains tribes** lived in the west central region. They relied on hunting herds of bison, buffalo, deer, elk, and antelope. Plains tribes included the Arapaho, Blackfoot, Cheyenne, Comanche, Crow, Osage, Pawnee, Sioux, and Wichita. Once horses were introduced to the continent, they became an important tool for the plains tribes.

Pueblo tribes lived in the southwestern United States and northern Mexico. They lived in houses made of adobe, which is a sun-dried clay brick. *Pueblo* is Spanish for "village." Pueblo tribes included the Apache, Hopi, Navajo, Yuma, and Zuni.

The **Pacific Northwest tribes** included the Chinook, Haida, Kwakiutl, Nootka, and Tlingit. The men were hunters and fishers, and the women gathered seeds, berries, and nuts for food.

The **California tribes** of Chumash, Karok, Maidu, Miwok, Pomo, and Yahi are also known as "seed gatherers of the desert." Their diets included berries, nuts, seeds, and roots. They were known for their basket weavers.

The **Great Basin and Plateau tribes** of the Flathead, Nez Percé, Paiute, Shoshone, Spokane, and Yakima lived in the west central region of what is now the United States and Canada.

The **Southeast tribes** of Alabama, Atakapa, Caddo, Catawba, Cherokee, Chickasaw, Choctaw, Natchez, Seminole, and Ticucua lived in what is now the southern and southeastern United States.

Mexican tribes included the Coahujltec, Concho, Lagunero, Seri, Yaqui, and the ancient Aztecs, Olmecs, and Toltecs. **Central America** is the home of the Mixtec, Tarascan, and Zapotec, as well as the ancient Mayan culture.

Mayan ruins

World Geography Puzzles — North America

North America: Native Americans (cont.)

Directions: Use the clues below to fill in the crossword puzzle with names and locations of Native American tribes. You may need to use the Internet or other resources to identify the tribes.

ACROSS
1. The Shoshone are one of the ____ ____ and Plateau tribes of the west central United States and Canada.
4. The ____ are one of the Pueblo tribes.
6. One of the California tribes of seed gatherers
8. An Algonquian-speaking Woodland tribe
9. This tribe, along with others in the Southeast, were forced to move to Indian Territory in the 1830s.
10. The ____ were one of the ancient tribes of Central America that built huge temple pyramids.
12. One of the Iroquois-speaking Woodland tribes
14. The Tlingit are one of the ____ ____ tribes where totem poles are common.
15. Spanish Conquistadors defeated the ____ tribe in Mexico.

DOWN
2. The ____ are one of the Southeast tribes who live mainly in Florida.
3. One of the Plains tribes that depended on hunting bison and deer
5. Northern Hunters, such as the Aleuts, are located in the ____ and subarctic regions.
6. These tribes were known for their basket weavers.
7. The ____ were an ancient tribe that lived in Mexico.
8. ____ tribes, such as the Sioux and Arapaho, relied on horses to help them hunt bison and move their families from summer to winter locations.
10. The Yaqui were one of the tribes located in ____.
11. Pueblo tribes make their houses out of this.
13. This tribe is also known as Eskimo.

World Geography Puzzles North America

Name: _____ Date: _____

North America: Regions

A region is an area that shares common physical or human characteristics with another place. For example, the United States and Canada share the same language, as well as sharing the Rocky Mountains. Northwest Mexico and the southwestern United States share a region of mountainous deserts.

Directions: Use the clues below to unscramble the names of regions in North America. These may be climate, political, physical, or human regions. Use the Internet or other resources if you need help.

1. EWN LDNENAG _____ Political region of the United States that includes Massachusetts, Vermont, Maine, and Connecticut

2. ETRDNAEERMANI _____ Climate found from 30°N to 40°N mostly in California

3. ATREG SIALPN _____ Grassland area in the middle of the continent in Canada and the United States

4. CRTOLAPI INAR TFROSE _____ Much of the east coast of Central America is this type of climate.

5. STRU ELBT _____ Area of the northeastern and midwestern United States where heavy industries used to be dominant but where the economy has since declined

6. ARDNTU _____ Climate type found in the far north of Canada

7. VIREARI _____ Coastal region of Mexico known for its resorts

8. RGATE SABNI _____ Region between the Wasatch Range and the Sierra Nevada Mountains where the rivers cannot drain to an ocean

9. BACIENABR _____ Region of islands and sea in the tropical zone between the United States and South America

10. NUS LTBE _____ States with warm, mild climates where many senior citizens retire

11. MHUDI NENCTONATIL _____ This climate region of the United States features warm summers and cold, snowy winters.

12. MITARSMIE _____ Region that includes the Canadian provinces of New Brunswick, Nova Scotia, and Prince Edward Island

World Geography Puzzles South America

Name: _____ Date: _____

South America: Locations of Major Cities

Directions: Location is the position of a place on Earth's surface. The absolute location is the latitude and longitude coordinates of a place. Using an atlas or the Internet, find the absolute locations below and fill in the name of the city at that location in the crossword puzzle. Coordinates may vary slightly from atlas to atlas.

ACROSS
2. 52°S, 68°W
4. 5°N, 52°W
5. 10°N, 67°W
6. 31°S, 58°W
7. 0°, 79°W
10. 3°N, 55°W
13. 6°N, 57°W
15. 10°N, 76°W
16. 3°S, 60°W
18. 24°S, 47°W
19. 17°S, 68°W
21. 2°S, 80°W
23. 8°N, 58°W
24. 12°S, 77°W
25. 23°S, 43°W
26. 11°N, 72°W
27. 5°N, 74°W

DOWN
1. 24°S, 70°W
2. 8°S, 35°W
3. 53°S, 71°W
5. 32°S, 64°W
8. 33°S, 71°W
9. 19°S, 65°W
11. 27°S, 55°W
12. 34°S, 58°W
14. 4°N, 52°W
16. 35°S, 56°W
17. 16°S, 48°W
20. 25°S, 57°W
22. 14°S, 72°W

CD-404133 © Mark Twain Media, Inc., Publishers   34

World Geography Puzzles — South America

South America: Physical Features

Directions: Use the clues below and an atlas or the Internet to find the names of physical features in South America. Write the names on the blanks provided. Then unscramble the circled letters to find a hidden word.

1. The world's longest mountain chain, located along the west coast of South America

2. Point at the southern tip of South America

3. South America's largest lake, located in Venezuela

4. The world's highest waterfall

5. Mountain that is the Western Hemisphere's highest point

6. The world's highest navigable lake, located on the border of Bolivia and Peru

7. River with more tributaries, more water volume, and larger drainage area than any other in the world

8. Desert in Chile with some of the driest land on Earth

9. High, cool plateau where most of Bolivia's people live

10. Large estuary where the Paraná and Uruguay Rivers flow in to the Atlantic between Argentina and Uruguay

11. Extinct volcano in Peru that is the second-highest point in the Western Hemisphere

12. Water passage between the South American mainland and Tierra del Fuego

13. Unscramble the circled letters to find the name for a group of islands on Chile's Pacific coast.

___ ___ ___ ___ ___ ___ ___ ___ ___ ___ ___ ___ de los Chonos

World Geography Puzzles   South America

Name: _____ Date: _____

South America: Plants, Animals, and Resources

Directions: Find and circle the plants, animals, resources, and industries of South America in the word search puzzle below.

```
G N K Z F G T A C T M X N G Y V I C U N A B Y L Z R M
K L Y M I I Z E N N R R T B M R W T O L E C O K K N T
R E L N M N S S E A M K M L N Q R K L L X F Q L Y J Q
E E M X F K C H A C K M W C V B V K L N K J J K B Z
S C Z H V P N H M N A O F E E B T D J H D L R M T K P
I I C T N K A L M E A R N P M R Q T R R N D K W C Z B
O R T O F P T D W T A N A D E B M Z D N O F D L O G S
T T V L L W U H G B H L A P A V Z G R N T T H N J P A
R C K S Y W R Q B G L P P B L C L T I Y T H X H E G N
O E J H I G A Y Y J M O I W Q P A T W Q O C K C K N D
T L M U N L L K E K C L K R E H E M G L C C T R T J E
S E Q M G F G R E B F R N T A L M K U C R A I P A A A
O O L B F X A R F F M L R P G N H W A P C P K G C M N
G I Y O I M S J F G J O V A M A H C G L A K U H M A C
A L P L S A X F O M L Z E Q C D A A E T G A L M L L O
P S N D H N G J C E L Y Y A L O M D N K R R G T R L N
A E T T K U G D U D P R P N V J B K Q D N V M L R T D
L E K P L F K M L R M L Y F R E T A E T N A L A R N O
A D X E G A W Z A D A A L N A B A U X I T E G K W E R
G T N N J C M H A D R A N R D O L P H I N U V E X L N
L T M G Q T Y W F R M R M A G L V P G T S N P R L I J
L H O U M U R X Q I A T E R T T W I Y L E A D O H D K
W M N I J R Z J N L S B R V P E G N A M I A C N Q O C
G D K N K I W G Q Z R H Y R L U E K K Z T N G O J C P
D R E V L N O C K F L M I P A I F W M D R C R R F O M
X K Y L L G R H E A F M V N A N S D V G V K M I P R R
A G R I C U L T U R E D A T G C T W A C A M B R Z C X
```

AGRICULTURE	CROCODILE	IGUANA	PETROLEUM
ALPACA	DOLPHIN	IRON ORE	PIRANHA
ANACONDA	ELECTRIC EEL	JAGUAR	PUMA
ANDEAN CONDOR	FISHING	LEAD	RHEA
ANTEATER	FISH MEAL	LLAMA	SILVER
BANANAS	FLAMINGO	MACAW	SLOTH
BAUXITE	FLYING FISH	MANATEE	SPECTACLED BEAR
BEEF	GALAPAGOS	MANUFACTURING	SUGAR
CACAO	TORTOISE	MONKEY	TAPIR
CAIMAN	GOLD	NATURAL GAS	TIN
CAPYBARA	HARPY EAGLE	OCELOT	VICUNA
COFFEE	HUMBOLDT	OILSEED	ZINC
COPPER	PENGUIN	PARAKEET	
COTTON			

South America: Colonial Settlement

The settlement of South America has depended on the movement of people, goods, and ideas across the land from North America and across the ocean from Europe and Africa. Ancestors of Native Americans crossed a narrow bridge of land between what is now Alaska and Siberia thousands of years ago. Over the centuries, the Native Americans populated all of North, Central, and South America.

In the Andes Mountains, a sophisticated Native American group called the Inca thrived and created a huge empire. The lands once controlled by the Inca now make up the nations of Peru, Ecuador, and Bolivia. They had major cities and a road system of over 19,300 km (12,000 miles). They developed terrace farming and created large irrigation systems.

Just like North America, South America was explored and conquered by Europeans. People from Spain, Portugal, and other European countries took over the land, some of which had been inhabited by Native Americans for centuries. In the 1500s, Spanish soldiers, called **Conquistadors**, conquered much of the continent. They came in search of gold and other riches. They enslaved much of the native population and also brought slaves from Africa to work in the mines and on plantations.

Through the years, much mixing of South America's ethnic groups occurred. **Mestizo** is the name given to a large part of the population who are descended from the Native Americans, the Spanish, and the Portuguese. **Mulatto** is the term for those of mixed African and European descent. Today, most of the Native Americans live in the highlands of the Andes Mountains. Spanish descendants are common in Argentina and Uruguay. Portuguese descendants are most common in Brazil. Many immigrants from other European and Asian countries have since joined the early Spanish and Portuguese settlers.

Most South Americans speak the language of the European country that once ruled the area in which they live. For example, Brazil was once a colony of Portugal, so today most Brazilians speak Portuguese. Most of the other South American countries were once dominated by Spain, so Spanish is widely spoken on the continent. The Dutch founded what is now Guyana in 1581, but the British took over the colony in 1831, so English is the official language there. The opposite happened in Suriname, with the Dutch taking over from the British in 1667. The French colonized the area now called French Guiana, so French is the main language there. There are many Native Americans in South America, especially in the highlands of Bolivia, Peru, Paraguay, and Chile, who still speak the languages of their ancestors, such as Quechua and Aymara. Most of the colonies became independent countries in the early 1800s; however, Suriname became independent in 1975, and French Guiana is still an overseas department of France.

The majority of South America's population lives close to the coasts. Some of the world's largest cities, such as Rio de Janeiro, São Paulo, and Buenos Aires, are on the Atlantic coast. Mountain valleys and plateaus, such as the Vale of Chile and the Altiplano of Bolivia, are also centers of population. Because much of the continent is covered in rough mountainous terrain or dense rain forests, railroads and highways have not been developed as much as they have in the United States. Using the different waterways in South America, such as the Amazon and the Paraná Rivers, the people have been able to move goods and ideas into otherwise unreachable areas of the continent.

World Geography Puzzles   South America

Name: _____ Date: _____

South America: Colonial Settlement (cont.)

Directions: Use the clues and an atlas or the Internet to help you unscramble the words below that are related to the colonial settlement of South America.

1. South American country that is still a part of a European country   HRFCNE ANIAUG
   _____

2. Large country colonized by the Portuguese   RLBIZA
   _____

3. Slaves from this continent were brought to work in South American mines and on plantations.   IFRCAA
   _____

4. How the ancestors of the Native Americans came to North and South America   DANL EBGRDI
   _____

5. Official language of Guyana   SLNIHEG
   _____

6. How most people and goods get to the interior of the South American continent   EWSAWARYT
   _____

7. One of the major cities on the Atlantic coast of South America   NUBESO IARSE
   _____

8. Spanish soldiers who conquered the Americas   DCSNROUTQSOIA
   _____

9. Native Americans who created a huge empire in Peru, Ecuador, and Bolivia   CNAI
   _____

10. Where most of the Native Americans in South America live today   DSANE IMNUNASOT
    _____

11. Descendants of Europeans and Native Americans   ZESTSIOM
    _____

12. Took over Suriname from the British in 1667   TUCHD
    _____

World Geography Puzzles — South America

Name: _____ Date: _____

South America: Regions

Directions: Use the clues below and an atlas or the Internet to find words associated with South America's geographic and cultural regions. Fill in the crossword puzzle with the correct region words.

ACROSS

2. World's largest wetland, covering up to 195,000 sq. km (75,000 sq. mi.) in southwestern Brazil and parts of Bolivia and Paraguay
3. Most South American countries have _____ as their official language.
5. Central valley where most people in Chile live and where most of the crops are grown (three words)
7. Tropical grassy plains in Venezuela and Colombia drained by the Orinoco River and used for grazing cattle
8. Fertile plain in Argentina used for ranching and growing crops
9. Many South American countries have a large _____ population, who are people descended from Europeans and Native Americans.
12. Region of table-like mountains covered in rain forest across southern Venezuela, Guyana, Suriname, and French Guiana, and northern Brazil (two words)
13. Low hills and plateaus that cover much of southeastern Brazil (two words)
14. Fertile grassland between the Parana and Uruguay Rivers in Argentina

DOWN

1. The largest religious group in South America is _____ _____.
2. Brazil is the largest _____ speaking nation in the world.
4. Dry grassland in southern Argentina used mostly for grazing sheep
6. The coasts of Ecuador and Peru are chilled by the cold _____ or Peru Current, which also provides rich fising areas.
10. Dry, subtropical, forested, sparsely populated region in Paraguay, Bolivia, Argentina, and Brazil that is known for its quebracho trees (two words)
11. Tropical rain forest that covers most of the northern half of South America

World Geography Puzzles   Europe

Name: _____ Date: _____

Europe: Locations of Major Cities

Directions: Using an atlas or the Internet, find the absolute locations of the cities listed below, and write the latitude and longitude coordinates for each city on your own paper. Coordinates may vary slightly from atlas to atlas. Then find and circle the cities in the word search puzzle. Words can go horizontally, vertically, and diagonally in all eight directions.

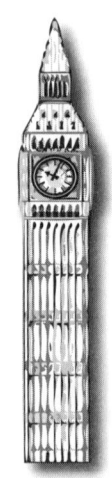

```
M A D R E T S M A F K C R Y L C R L B D
V C H I S I N A U F O D U B L I N J E M
A N A V E R E Y C P F K J R V S D A L D
V A T H E N S C E Q I N L L N T K G G B
A K V W N Z T N M V L M P L Y O L I R G
L V E I K N H M A M M I N S K C L R A G
S K S M E A I J W O C S O M G K D B D R
I L L K G N K L T B I L I S I H N W E U
T F E E O Y N D L S A B Z B J O O D H O
A B N S E P N A A A Z I U K L L D I T B
R L E R S O J R L S T D F R Y M N R L M
B O B R B U A E I Y A N Q O T T O D J E
Q L S S G J R R B P L P H N S F L A U X
M M I L E A A B E Y T E H E Y F S M B U
B L N V O P Z S R P L Z R W W U F Y L L
E Y O X T J T W N S K A P H I A N Z J N
R P R A G U E Y I R H R V N W B R T A Y
L R V Z M J N N M C O J L K P V A S N H
I H X J Y N K M U M R I R X L F T K A Z
N G T T R I C B E G V M E N A R I T U W
```

1. AMSTERDAM
2. ATHENS
3. BAKU
4. BELGRADE
5. BERLIN
6. BERN
7. BRATISLAVA
8. BRUSSELS
9. BUCHAREST
10. BUDAPEST
11. CHISINAU
12. COPENHAGEN
13. DUBLIN
14. HELSINKI
15. KIEV
16. LISBON
17. LJUBLJANA
18. LONDON
19. LUXEMBOURG
20. MADRID
21. MINSK
22. MOSCOW
23. OSLO
24. PARIS
25. PRAGUE
26. REYKJAVIK
27. RIGA
28. ROME
29. SARAJEVO
30. SKOPJE
31. SOFIA
32. STOCKHOLM
33. TALLINN
34. TBILISI
35. TIRANE
36. VIENNA
37. VILNIUS
38. WARSAW
39. YEREVAN
40. ZAGREB

CD-404133 © Mark Twain Media, Inc., Publishers   40

World Geography Puzzles — Europe

Name: _____ Date: _____

Europe: Physical Features

Directions: Using an atlas or the Internet, find the European physical features listed below. Then label them with the letter of the correct type of feature.

I. Island
R. River
M. Mountain Range
S. Sea
P. Peninsula

_____ 1. Adriatic
_____ 2. Aegean
_____ 3. Alps
_____ 4. Apennines
_____ 5. Azov
_____ 6. Balkan
_____ 7. Baltic
_____ 8. Barents
_____ 9. Black
_____ 10. Carpathians
_____ 11. Caspian
_____ 12. Caucasus
_____ 13. Corsica
_____ 14. Crete
_____ 15. Crimean
_____ 16. Danube
_____ 17. Dnepr
_____ 18. Don
_____ 19. Douro
_____ 20. Ebro

_____ 21. Elbe
_____ 22. Great Britain
_____ 23. Iberian
_____ 24. Iceland
_____ 25. Ionian
_____ 26. Ireland
_____ 27. Irish
_____ 28. Italian
_____ 29. Jutland
_____ 30. Ligurian
_____ 31. Loire
_____ 32. Kjölen
_____ 33. Kola
_____ 34. Majorca
_____ 35. Mediterranean
_____ 36. North
_____ 37. Norwegian
_____ 38. Novaya Zemlya
_____ 39. Oder
_____ 40. Peloponnesus

_____ 41. Pennines
_____ 42. Po
_____ 43. Pripyat
_____ 44. Pyrenees
_____ 45. Rhine
_____ 46. Rhodes
_____ 47. Rhône
_____ 48. Sardinia
_____ 49. Scandinavian
_____ 50. Seine
_____ 51. Sicily
_____ 52. Sjælland
_____ 53. Svalbard
_____ 54. Tagus
_____ 55. Thames
_____ 56. Tyrrhenian
_____ 57. Ural
_____ 58. Urals
_____ 59. Volga
_____ 60. White

Europe: Plants, Animals, and Resources

Directions: Using the code key below, decode the missing words in the paragraphs.

AGRICULTURE is one of Europe's major industries. Dairy and meat products are dominant in **WESTERN** Europe. Cattle, goats, pigs, sheep, and **POULTRY** are common throughout the continent. In eastern Europe, crops such as **GRAINS** and vegetables are more important. Wheat, **OLIVES**, grapes, and citrus fruits are the major crops in the Mediterranean.

Scandinavia and Russia have a large **FORESTRY** industry. This includes **WOODPULP** for papermaking as well as lumber and other **BUILDING** products. **CORK** is harvested in Spain and Portugal.

Britain, **DENMARK**, Norway, Poland, and Spain all have major fishing industries. Cod, haddock, herring, **MACKEREL**, and sardines are caught in the ocean waters. **SALMON** are found in the rivers. Sturgeon that live in the Black and Caspian Seas are a source of **CAVIAR**.

The **INDUSTRIAL** Revolution began in Europe, and major production centers developed in Great Britain, Germany, France, Poland, and the Ukraine. Industries take advantage of the large quantities of coal, iron ore, **BAUXITE**, copper, manganese, **NICKEL**, and potash mined in Europe. Oil and **NATURAL GAS** are available in southern Russia and the North Sea. While manufacturing has decreased over the last half century, Europe's chemical and **ELECTRONIC** industries have increased greatly.

Since Europe has become so developed and heavily populated, many species of wild animals have become reduced in numbers or **EXTINCT**. Deer, bear, elk, and **WOLVES** are only found in northern Scandinavia and Russia. **CHAMOIS** and ibex are found in the Pyrenees and Alps. Herds of domesticated reindeer live in the **LAPLAND** region of Scandinavia. Birds commonly found in Europe include eagles, falcons, finches, nightingales, owls, pigeons, **STORKS**, and swans.

A	B	C	D	E	F	G	H	I	J	K	L	M	N	O	P	Q	R	S	T	U	V	W	X	Y	Z
11	5	21	18	4	9	12	23	8	22	17	3	24	7	16	25	1	19	26	2	14	6	10	20	13	15

Europe: Movement of People, Goods, and Ideas

Europe is a perfect example of how geography can affect the movement of people, goods, and ideas, both within the continent and out into the rest of the world. Some areas were isolated by the difficulty of traveling over mountain ranges, such as the Alps. Other areas had access to trade and movement by using the many navigable rivers and developing fleets of ships that could sail the seas and oceans. The Rhine River in Germany and the Netherlands is one of the busiest rivers in the world for transporting goods. The Danube River crosses a large stretch of the the interior of the European continent before emptying into the Black Sea. From there, ships can make their way to the Mediterranean Sea and the open ocean. Today, the continent is also linked by an extensive system of railroads.

The original Greek **city-states**, with each city being self-governing, were formed because it was difficult to unite all the Greek people when the cities were separated by mountains and seas. However, Alexander the Great was able to spread the Greek language and culture throughout much of the Middle East by sailing and marching his army through Egypt, Persia, and as far as India.

Throughout Europe's history, the rise of kingdoms and empires led to armies being moved into areas to take control of land and to change or move borders. As each civilization rose in importance, some people were forced out and others moved in. Each group of people brought customs, religions, languages, and systems of government that dominated and sometimes blended with the previous group's way of life. The Romans pushed north into the Germanic lands. Then Germanic tribes pushed south to break up the Roman Empire. Germanic and Scandinavian tribes also moved into the British Isles, followed by the Normans from France. These groups developed strong common cultures that became the basis of national identities. Unfortunately, these strong national identities often led to confrontation and more wars. England and France fought a long series of wars, but they finally came together as allies to fight Germany in two world wars.

Since Europe is located so close to Asia and Africa and the open sea lanes to the Americas, opportunities for movement have been the greatest in the world. Europeans have been able to spread ideas that have shaped and influenced the modern world. The European voyages of discovery, exploration, religious missionary efforts, and colonization helped to spread European ideas, religious beliefs, traditions, and languages around the globe. North America, South America, and Australia are inhabited largely by descendents who speak European languages. Africa was also heavily colonized by European nations until the African nations gained their independence in the twentieth century.

There are over 50 different languages spoken in Europe, but most of them belong to the **Indo-European language family**. The three branches of this family are **Balto-Slavic**, **Germanic**, and **Romantic**. The Slavic-based languages of eastern Europe include Russian, Czech, Slovak, Polish, and Serbo-Croatian. Germanic languages spoken mostly in northern Europe include English, German, Dutch, Danish, Norwegian, Swedish, and Icelandic. Romantic-based languages of southern Europe include Italian, French, Spanish, Portuguese, and Romanian. Chances are good if your family came from Europe, you speak one of these Indo-European languages.

World Geography Puzzles

Europe

Name: _____ Date: _____

Europe: Movement of People, Goods, and Ideas (cont.)

Directions: Use the clues below to complete the crossword puzzle about the movement of people, goods, and ideas in and out of Europe.

ACROSS

1. He spread Greek culture through much of the Middle East (three words)
4. Modern ground transportation that connects much of Europe today
7. River in Germany and the Netherlands used for transporting goods
8. Because some areas were isolated by the difficulty of traveling over ____ ranges, they formed their own governments and cultures.
10. When a parent country sends a group of people to live in a new territory while retaining ties to the parent country
13. These people tried to expand their empire by pushing north into the Germanic lands.
14. German and ____ tribes moved into the British Isles.
15. England and ____ were bitter enemies who fought a long series of wars.

DOWN

2. North America, South America, and ____ are inhabited largely by descendents of Europeans.
3. When groups developed strong common cultures, it became the basis for ____ identities.
5. ____ languages include Italian, French, and Spanish.
6. Most of the languages spoken in Europe belong to the ____-____ language family.
9. Self-governing unit in ancient Greece (hyphenated word)
11. The European voyages of ____, exploration, and colonization helped to spread European ideas around the globe.
12. River that crosses Europe west to east and empties into the Black Sea

CD-404133 © Mark Twain Media, Inc., Publishers

World Geography Puzzles

Europe

Name: _____ Date: _____

Europe: Regions

Directions: Use the clues below and an atlas or the Internet to help you unscramble the names of various regions in Europe. These may be cultural, political, geographical, or climate regions.

1. Mountainous region of France, Switzerland, Germany, Austria, and Italy known for winter sports and picturesque views

   AILNPE
   _____

2. Southeastern region of Europe that includes Albania, Greece, Croatia, Serbia, and Bosnia and Herzegovina; has seen war recently due to ethnic and religious differences

   SANAKBL
   _____

3. Region of southeast Germany known for its forested mountains, elaborate castles, wood carvers, chocolate makers, and beer breweries

   AVRAABI
   _____

4. Climate region in southern Europe that enjoys hot, sunny summers and mild, rainy winters

   TRIAREAEDMNNE
   _____

5. A group of European countries that have signed economic, scientific, and political agreements to make trade and collaboration among the nations easier

   EOPRAUNE   OIUNN
   _____

6. Region of France known for its sparkling wine

   AGCENMHAP
   _____

7. The former Soviet republics that are now the independent countries of Estonia, Latvia, and Lithuania

   IBCALT   INOTSNA
   _____

8. Resort area on the Mediterranean coastline of France

   FENRCH   IIAREVR
   _____

9. The northern countries of Norway, Sweden, Finland, and Denmark; once the home of the Vikings

   SADICNAVNAI
   _____

10. River valley between Mainz and Bonn in Germany known for its many castles and vineyards

    HRNIE   LVAYLE
    _____

11. England, Wales, Scotland, Northern Ireland, Ireland, and the adjacent islands

    TBSRHII   ESISL
    _____

12. Most-populated and southern-most region of Spain that includes the city of Seville and the palace of Alhambra at Granada

    AAALDNUSI
    _____

World Geography Puzzles   Africa

Name: _____ Date: _____

Africa: Locations of Major Cities

Directions: Using an atlas or the Internet, find the absolute locations of the cities listed below, and write the latitude and longitude coordinates for each city on your own paper. Coordinates may vary slightly from atlas to atlas. Then find and circle the cities in the word search puzzle. Words can go horizontally, vertically, and diagonally in all eight directions.

```
F I R N J T M G H X P D W N B M T K Y W I X Z K Q K P N B I S S A U C
L U M C M Q Y J X W J U R B R Q H Q R D T N Q V N L D G X B M A B M M
X G N R K H M Q O K K N R N T E R X K K U W P N G D C C J W R N M V T
J N M Z Z R Z N L H T L M E N H Q A A E O O M X E R J N Q C K I X N M
K A R F N A J D I B A L M A S F T N N O B T R G V M Y A C M N A M Q N
W B Z H G T X N X K U N B V M A M T O H I E T N T R O A M R T M B X S
K T P Y L L V T O A H A N Y D H M A C D J P N B K K R L Q E T E T O F
E W G N O L I L N U B A X E W N G N N D A A I V O R N O M N Y G Y H
Y V G L N X R D P M A B B L S D T A R I X C K Z P T C L T G M A A F Y
Z R T K T T A N K L D K N U R B B N T W K M D K O G M F D B L L A F N
R L T W R P X Y W E P A C K J N U A Z X R G Z J R T J V U G G V D T P
K I N S H A S A X R T A R H W A D R H B K N L D I T R J V I H C D N J
Y N B T R K H T H A U R C E O C L I G G H D W J A S U I E N W W I X X
E V J P C M Q X E R K O N N S T V V P N A V L X C M I R P N N R S Q F
N D V L F P R N P A Q R G R A S T O T R R J X Z B L S N R O N X A K R
J W N G L V O O Q H T M T U Y L A G V K T L F U F R F Y U M L E B R E
L M R U Q R R C A K A S U L O Z B L B K O Q R P M Y D F U T L I A D E
T P R D O T F L T P M G C K M D X A A F U A K L G K F H F A G L B X T
N T W B O A D F J N L L L P Y K A L S A M P W A R C S V A Q F D A Z O
Y K A N R L Y K B N A I R O B I T G J A M X L B O I K I C R X H V B W
D G O R R R C N R A K A D G Z H A K C A Y B D M U W T N G P A N N
R V B R A Z Z A V I L L E X T A L N Q U P D A A R N T G J D K M M P B
O Q Q J Z M Q L U J N A B L K L K J V M O L G C H W H Z R M A P U T O
J V Q C X L I B R E V I L L E I H K A R A O N G H M C K M K V D M R X
D H F K Z Q B T C F R B P T K R K K Z M M R T R M C Z N O Y T H T Y C
```

1. ABIDJAN	11. BRAZZAVILLE	21. FREETOWN	31. LILONGWE	41. NAIROBI
2. ABUJA	12. BUJUMBURA	22. GABORONE	32. LOME	42. N'DJAMENA
3. ACCRA	13. CAIRO	23. HARARE	33. LUANDA	43. NIAMEY
4. ADDIS ABABA	14. CAPE TOWN	24. JOHANNESBURG	34. LUSAKA	44. NOUAKCHOTT
5. ALGIERS	15. CASABLANCA	25. KAMPALA	35. MALABO	45. OUAGADOUGOU
6. ANTANANARIVO	16. CONAKRY	26. KHARTOUM	36. MAPUTO	46. PORTO-NOVO
7. BAMAKO	17. DAKAR	27. KIGALI	37. MASERU	47. TRIPOLI
8. BANGUI	18. DARESSALAAM	28. KINSHASA	38. MBABANE	48. TUNIS
9. BANJUL	19. DJIBOUTI	29. LAGOS	39. MOGADISHU	49. WINDHOEK
10. BISSAU	20. EL AAIUN	30. LIBREVILLE	40. MONROVIA	50. YAOUNDE

World Geography Puzzles   Africa

Name: _____ Date: _____

Africa: Physical Features

Directions: Using the clues below and an atlas or the Internet, complete the crossword puzzle with the names of the African physical features described.

ACROSS
4. Large swamp located in northern Botswana
8. This river flows along the boundary of Zambia and Zimbabwe and east across Mozambique.
11. This lake is located in the Great Rift Valley on the border between Tanzania and the Democratic Republic of the Congo. (two words)
13. This peak is the highest volcano in Kenya. (two words)
14. This large lake, named for an English queen, is located on the equator on the border between Kenya, Uganda, and Tanzania. (two words)
18. Beginning in Uganda and Ethiopa, this famous river flows north through Sudan and Egypt to the Mediterranean Sea at Alexandria.
19. The _____ Mountains are found along the southeast coast of South Africa.
20. This river starts in the highlands of Guinea and then flows northeast and south to empty into the Atlantic at the Gulf of Guinea.

DOWN
1. This lake is located on the border between Chad, Niger, and Nigeria. (two words)
2. This long valley extends along the eastern side of Africa. On the valley floor are several long slender lakes. (three words)
3. This famous African mountain peak is located in Tanzania, just south of the border with Kenya.
5. This desert located in Botswana is the home of the Hottentots, a nomadic people who have learned to survive in this very dry climate.
6. This is the world's largest desert. It is home to the veiled Tuareg tribe.
7. Peninsula bordered by the Gulf of Suez on the west and the Gulf of Aqaba on the east
9. This mountain group is located between Lake Albert and Lake Edward.
10. Desert located in eastern Libya and western Egypt
12. This desert extends along the entire coast of Namibia.
15. The _____ Mountains are found in Morocco and Algeria.
16. This river flows from the Drakensberg Mountains west across South Africa to the Atlantic.
17. This river flows west through the heavily forested Democratic Republic of the Congo and on to the Atlantic Ocean.

World Geography Puzzles Africa

Name: _____ Date: _____

Africa: Plants, Animals, and Resources

Directions: Africa is perhaps the richest continent in natural resources. It contains many of the world's largest mineral resources, and it has a great diversty of animal life. Listed below are just a few of Africa's resources, industries, plants, and animals. Fit them into the puzzle using the given letters as clues. The last letter of one word will be the first letter of the next word. The words will go down one column and up the next in a continuous line. The first word is done for you.

AARDVARK
ADDER
AGOUTI
ANTELOPE
CACAO
COBRA
DIAMONDS
EGRET
ELEPHANT
FENNEC
GOLD
GIRAFFE
GORILLA
HEDGEHOG
IBIS
KENAF
LION
MAHOGANY
MANUFACTURING
MICA
MILLET
NATURAL GAS
OLIVE OIL
OSTRICH
PETROLEUM
RADIUM
RHINOCEROS
SALT
SAND VIPER
SHEEP
SUBSISTENCE FARMING
TEA
TENREC
TITANIUM
TOBACCO
URANIUM
YAMS

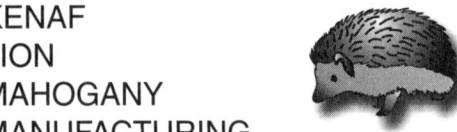

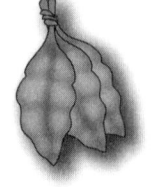

1 U				25		35	
R		G	16				I
A	10	15		I			
N			17		E		
I	9 N			26			
U			24		O		
2 M		D		34	36		
	H						
		14					
				27	33	37	
		18	D				
A	8					T	
				32			
3			23	28			
	11	19		S			
	E						
4							
	12	N		31			
7 A							
		20	29	L			
5							
	6 O		H				
T		22	G				
		21		30			
	13	D					

CD-404133 © Mark Twain Media, Inc., Publishers 48

Africa: Climate

Africa has a variety of climate conditions. The continent has few mountain ranges acting as barriers, and several ocean currents help maintain stable climates throughout much of the continent.

Average African temperatures range from 94°F (34°C) in Ethiopia to 51°F (11°C) in Morocco. The average precipitation ranges from 404 inches (10,261 mm) in Cameroon to 0.1 inches (2.5 mm) in the Sudan. In general, regions to the north of the equator have their rainy season from April to September. South of the equator, the rainy season is from October to March. Regions near the equator have year-round rain.

Africa's mildest climate conditions are along the northwest and southwest edges of the continent. These **Mediterranean** climate zones have mild temperatures, wet winters, and dry summers.

The central part of the continent and much of the island of Madagascar include **tropical rain forests**. In the rain forest areas, the average temperature is 80°F (27°C). The average rainfall each year is 70 inches (1,778 mm).

North and south of the rain forest area is a **tropical savanna** climate. A savanna is a hot region like a tropical forest; however, it only receives major rainfall for about half the year. The other half of the year is a dry season. Many of Africa's famous animals, such as lions, giraffe, elephants, and wildebeest, live in the grasslands of the savanna climate regions.

Farther away from the equator, both to the north and to the south, the regions have a drier climate known as a **steppe** climate zone. The rainfall in the steppe zone is about 15 inches (381 mm) per year. Most of the rain in the steppe arrives in one season.

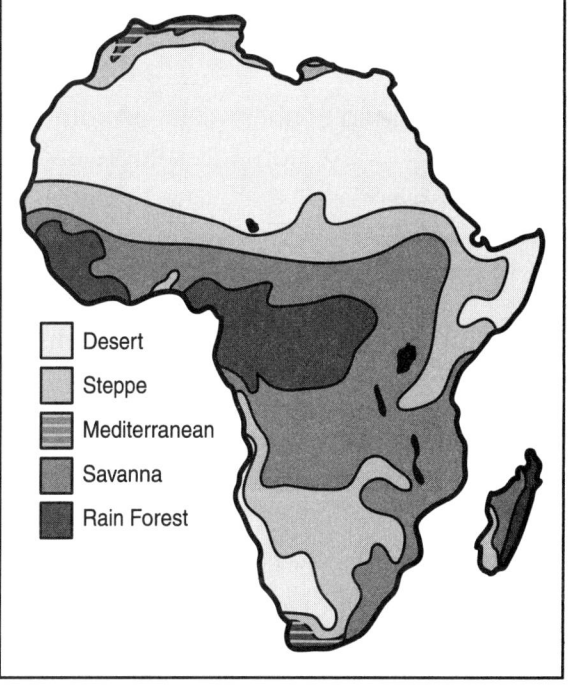

Africa is perhaps best known for its massive **desert** regions. In the Sahara, Horn, Kalahari, and Namib Deserts, the rainfall is less than 10 inches (254 mm) each year. The desert temperatures range from over 90°F (32°C) in the summer season to below freezing in the winter season.

Due to man's interaction with the environment, the Sahara Desert has actually gotten larger. **Desertification** is a term used to refer to those dry lands where the environment has been altered, with a resulting increase in the amount of desert. South of the Sahara Desert, a region known as the **Sahel** was a broad band of short grasses where nomadic people grazed their animals. Although the region was dry and the grasses were short, it did provide enough grazing for the animals. However, overgrazing in exceptionally dry years resulted in the destruction of the sparse short grasses. The winds blew away large amounts of topsoil, and the Sahel became a part of the Sahara Desert.

Africa: Climate (cont.)

Directions: Use the clues below and an atlas or the Internet to unscramble words associated with Africa's climates.

1. Climate just north and south of the rain forest that only receives rainfall for half the year — COLATRIP NSAAVNA _____

2. Climate zones on the northwest and southwest edges of the continent that have mild temperatures, wet winters, and dry summers — TENADEMIRANER _____

3. Broad band of short grasses south of the Sahara Desert where nomadic people once grazed their animals — LHEAS _____

4. This ranges from 404 inches (10,261 mm) in Cameroon to 0.1 inches (2.5 mm) in the Sudan. — TINOREIICPPAT _____

5. Climate regions that receive less than 10 inches (254 mm) of rainfall a year — SRSDTEE _____

6. This tropical climate region covers most of the central part of Africa and much of the island of Madagascar. — NIRA ORSFET _____

7. Refers to those dry lands where the environment has been altered and the land has been turned into desert — ITOITFSADNRIECE _____

8. Dry climate farther away from the equator with rain in only one season of the year — PTESEP _____

9. The _____ of the savanna are home to many of Africa's famous animals, such as lions and giraffe. — SGSDNALSAR _____

10. These help maintain stable climates thoughout much of the continent of Africa. — NOECA NRSRCETU _____

World Geography Puzzles
Africa

Name: _____ Date: _____

Africa: Regions of Conflict

Directions: Read the following paragraphs and use the code key below to decode the missing words.

Africa is a continent rich in resources, natural beauty, and diverse people, but the relatively young _____ (R M W V K V M W V M G) countries of Africa have struggled to provide stable governments and economies for their growing populations. Conflicts over limited resources, such as food and water, as well as between _____ (I V O R T R L F H) and ethnic groups, have led to thousands of deaths and millions of people fleeing from their homes. People who cross an _____ (R M G V I M Z G R L M Z O) border and seek protection from a government that is not their own are called refugees. Internally _____ (W R H K O Z X V W) people (IDP) are people who flee persecution by going to another part of the same country.

The most publicized conflict at this time is in the _____ (W Z I U F I) province of Sudan. Black Africans in the Darfur region claimed the Arab-led government was _____ (W R H X I R N R M Z G R M T) against them, so they formed armed groups to attack the government. Then, the government-backed militias called the _____ (Q Z M Q Z D R W) attacked the rebel groups and civilians in Darfur. They killed and terrorized men, women, and children, forcing millions of people (2.5 million by 2006) to flee across the border into _____ (X S Z W) or to scatter to other areas of _____ (H F W Z M). As many as 500,000 may have died from the fighting, as well as the _____ (N Z O M F G I R G R L M) and disease in the refugee camps.

Central and eastern Africa have some of the worst ongoing conflict in the world. By January 2009, the _____ (F M R G V W) _____ (M Z G R L M H) was supporting nearly 11 million refugees and IDPs in Burundi, Central African Republic, Chad, Congo, Democratic Republic of the Congo, _____ (V G S R L K R Z), Kenya, Somalia, Sudan, and Uganda.

Other areas of conflict include border disputes between Cameroon and Nigeria and between _____ (V I R G I V Z) and its neighbors. Zimbabwe has seen months of violence since the disputed _____ (V O V X G R L M) in March 2008. Civil wars, protests against _____ (X L I I F K G) governments, and violence against foreign-owned companies continue to make life uncertain and chaotic for people in many regions of Africa.

A	B	C	D	E	F	G	H	I	J	K	L	M	N	O	P	Q	R	S	T	U	V	W	X	Y	Z
Z	Y	X	W	V	U	T	S	R	Q	P	O	N	M	L	K	J	I	H	G	F	E	D	C	B	A

CD-404133 © Mark Twain Media, Inc., Publishers

World Geography Puzzles   Asia

Name: _____ Date: _____

Asia: Locations of Major Cities

Directions: Location is the position of a place on Earth's surface. The absolute location is the latitude and longitude coordinates of a place. Using an atlas or the Internet, find the absolute locations below and fill in the name of the city at that location in the crossword puzzle. Coordinates may vary slightly from atlas to atlas.

ACROSS
2. 38°N, 58°E
5. 34°N, 132°E
7. 29°N, 77°E
8. 47°N, 107°E
14. 25°N, 47°E
15. 16°N, 44°E
16. 31°N, 121°E
19. 5°N, 115°E
22. 23°N, 58°E
23. 35°N, 69°E
26. 25°N, 121°E
30. 35°N, 33°E
31. 40°N, 33°E
32. 43°N, 132°E
35. 24°N, 90°E
36. 32°N, 36°E
39. 15°N, 121°E
40. 14°N, 100°E
41. 25°N, 51°E
44. 12°N, 105°E
45. 3°N, 102°E
46. 39°N, 127°E
47. 34°N, 35°E
48. 21°N, 106°E

DOWN
1. 21°N, 40°E
3. 28°N, 90°E
4. 18°N, 103°E
6. 24°N, 54°E
9. 41°N, 69°E
10. 17°N, 96°E
11. 39°N, 69°E
12. 34°N, 73°E
13. 51°N, 72°E
17. 55°N, 83°E
18. 38°N, 127°E
20. 1°N, 104°E
21. 32°N, 35°E
23. 29°N, 48°E
24. 36°N, 51°E
25. 43°N, 75°E
27. 28°N, 85°E
28. 22°N, 114°E
29. 40°N, 116°E
33. 33°N, 36°E
34. 6°S, 107°E
37. 36°N, 140°E
38. 26°N, 51°E
40. 33°N, 44°E
42. 7°N, 80°E
43. 19°N, 73°E

CD-404133 © Mark Twain Media, Inc., Publishers   52

World Geography Puzzles   Asia

Name: _____ Date: _____

Asia: Physical Features

Directions: Use the clues below and an atlas or the Internet to come up with the words you must find in the word search puzzle on the next page. Fill in the blanks below, and then find and circle the words in the puzzle. Words can go horizontally, vertically, and diagonally in all eight directions.

1. Mountains that divide European Russia from Asian Russia _____
2. Cold desert in Mongolia and China _____
3. Major river of southeast Asia, flowing through Laos, Thailand, Vietnam, and Cambodia _____
4. Peninsula surrounded by the Red Sea, Gulf of Aden, Arabian Sea, Gulf of Oman, Persian Gulf, and the Mediterranean Sea _____
5. Mountains along the east coast of India _____
6. Longest river in China that enters the East China Sea near Shanghai _____
7. Desert in Turkmenistan _____
8. Mountains along Iran's border with Iraq and the Persian Gulf _____
9. Island divided among Malaysia, Indonesia, and Brunei _____
10. Russian peninsula that comes within a few miles of North America _____
11. River that flows through the center of Pakistan _____
12. Largest lake in the world (salt water) _____
13. Mountain range with some of the highest peaks in the world, located in Nepal, Bhutan, and along the border of India, Pakistan, and China _____
14. River that flows through Syria, into Iraq, and on to the Persian Gulf _____
15. Island at the southern tip of India _____
16. Desert in northern Iran on the Plateau of Iran _____
17. Mountains along the west coast of India _____
18. Desert on India's border with Pakistan _____
19. Largest freshwater lake and deepest lake in the world _____
20. Chinese river known as the Yellow River _____
21. Mountains along Iran's northern border with the Caspian Sea _____
22. Desert in China bordered by the Tien Shan on the north and the Altun Shan on the south _____
23. Peninsula in southeast Asia divided between Malaysia and Thailand _____
24. One of the two great rivers in Iraq on which Baghdad is located _____
25. Mountain range in northeast Afghanistan _____
26. This peninsula is sometimes called a subcontinent _____
27. Saltwater lake near the lowest point on Earth _____
28. River that flows across northern India east to the Bay of Bengal _____
29. Desert in Saudi Arabia known as the empty quarter _____
30. Mountains that extend through Kyrgistan into China _____

World Geography Puzzles　　　　　　　　　　　　　　　　　　　　　　　　　　Asia

Name: _____　Date: _____

Asia: Physical Features (cont.)

Directions: Find and circle the physical features from the previous page in the word search puzzle below. Words can go horizontally, vertically, and diagonally in all eight directions.

```
D H Z S R I L A N K A W H Q V G M Z G
N A I Z Q P Y M S E T A R H P U E B R
H A S N N L A E S D A E D P L T L O E
L U H H D A B C X C A S P I A N S E A
H G A S T U I R U B A L K H A L I N T
N N W N N E K B T R T A T S F H R R I
K O Q J G E K U A Y W R D B U Q D O N
V K M I K W I A S R K U A F W D T B D
H E D H N M K T V H A Y H E Z I N H I
I M G C A R A T H I K K S R B Q N I A
M M R K K M R D D A R T U O T A T K N
A R X U A D A Z L M E B G I I Y L G D
L V Y H M X K M T R L S G D N N H Q E
A Y K C A T U R N E E R N M H V P R S
Y A Q H L X M G D G I I B K B M T K E
A L M M K W H G N S Y A N G T Z E N R
S A V H A A K A J W G M Z A G R O S T
Q M L B T K G S T A H G N R E T S A E
Q X L S M F R F Y B Q M K B G F X T T
```

CD-404133 © Mark Twain Media, Inc., Publishers　　　　54

World Geography Puzzles   Asia

Name: _____ Date: _____

Asia: Plants, Animals, and Resources

Directions: Choose from the industries, resources, plants, and animals listed below to fill in the puzzle. Use the letters provided and the length of the word to help you find the correct words that fit in the puzzle. Not all the words will be used. The first one is done for you.

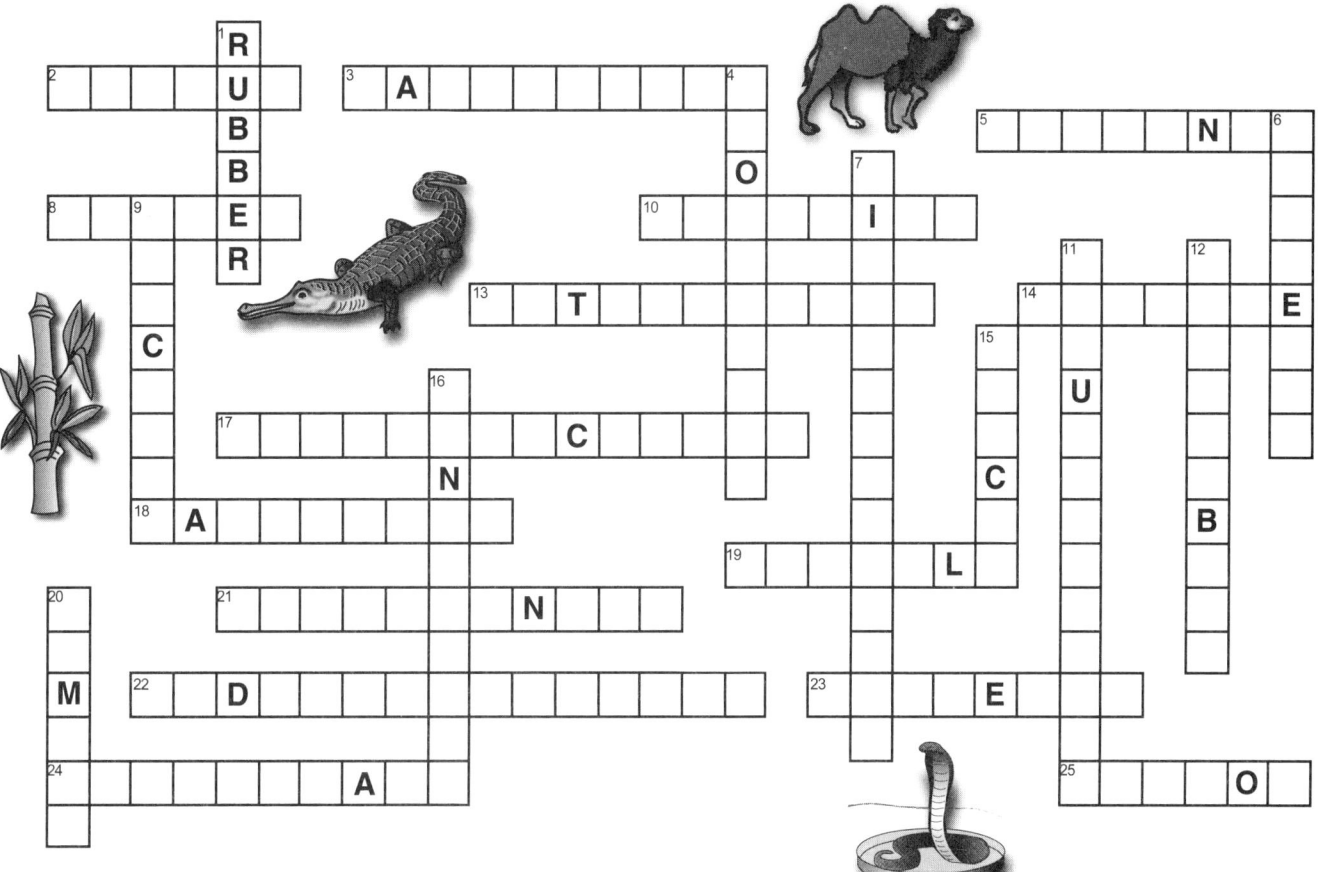

crude oil	timber	cattle	Indian elephants
natural gas	bamboo	fishing	Malay tapirs
coal	agriculture	manufacturing	water buffalo
iron ore	rice	automobiles	reindeer
bauxite	rubber	chemicals	Indian rhinoceroses
tin	palms	clothing	peacocks
diamonds	coconut	electronics	birds of paradise
sapphires	pineapples	orangutans	spoonbills
rubies	coffee	giant pandas	falcons
gold	cotton	snow leopards	fairy bluebirds
silver	peanuts	Komodo dragons	king cobras
copper	spices	yaks	vipers
lead	corn	gibbons	adders
uranium	soybeans	Siberian tigers	crocodiles
zinc	wheat	Bactrian camels	gavials
sulfur	swine	Bengal tigers	geckos
graphite	poultry		

World Geography Puzzles   Asia

Name: _____   Date: _____

Asia: Population Density

Directions: Find the population density (people per square kilometer) by dividing each country's population by its land area. Round to the nearest tenth.

	Country	Land Area (including indigenous waters)	Population (2006)	Population Density
1.	Russia	17,075,200	143,420,300	_____
2.	China	9,596,960	1,306,313,800	_____
3.	India	3,287,590	1,080,264,400	_____
4.	Kazakhstan	2,717,300	15,185,000	_____
5.	Saudi Arabia	1,960,582	26,417,600	_____
6.	Indonesia	1,919,440	241,973,900	_____
7.	Afghanistan	647,500	29,929,000	_____
8.	Japan	377,835	127,417,200	_____
9.	Laos	236,800	6,217,100	_____
10.	Israel	20,770	6,276,900	_____

Directions: Use the information above to help you label the graph below, putting the countries in the correct positions.

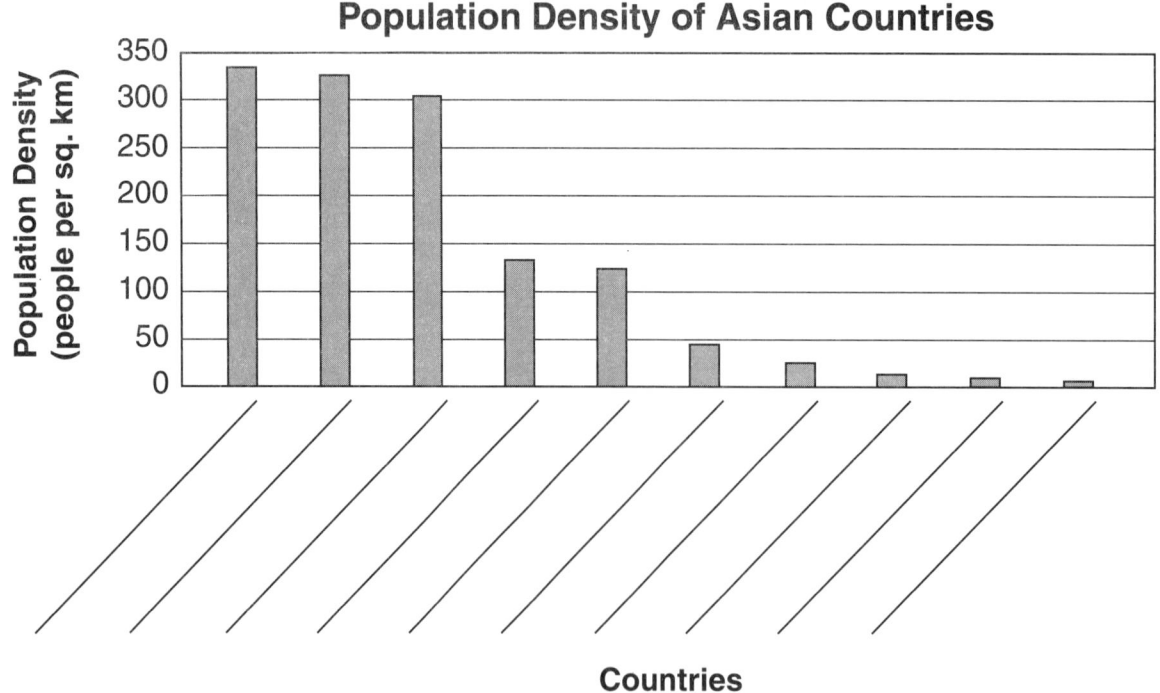

World Geography Puzzles　　　　　　　　　　　　　　　　　　　　　　　　　Asia

Name: _____ Date: _____

Asia: Regions

Directions: Use the clues below and an atlas or the Internet to unscramble words associated with Asia's political, cultural, and climate regions.

1. Asian region that went through a series of wars from the 1950s to 1970s; includes Vietnam, Cambodia, Myanmar, and Malaysia

   AESTOTSUH AIAS
   _____

2. Much of Indonesia is this type of climate region

   RTLAOIPC RNIA SREOFT
   _____

3. Russian Asia includes countries that used to be part of this Communist republic

   ETOIVS INONU
   _____

4. India is sometimes referred to as this

   NINUBTNOSECT
   _____

5. Region in southwest Asia that includes Arab nations, as well as Israel; an oil-rich region that is constantly in conflict

   EIDLMD AETS
   _____

6. Subarctic region of Russia where average winter temperatures are below -5°F (-20°C)

   REIBSIA
   _____

7. Region in southwest China on a high plateau that would like to be an independent country; its spiritual leader is called the Dalai Lama

   EIBTT
   _____

8. Region that includes India, Bangladesh, Nepal, Bhutan, and Pakistan

   UHTOS AASI
   _____

9. This region along the Mediterranean coast has sites sacred to Christians, Muslims, and Jews

   LYOH NDLA
   _____

10. Includes China, Mongolia, Japan, Taiwan, the Philippines, and North and South Korea

    RFA SETA
    _____

CD-404133 © Mark Twain Media, Inc., Publishers　　　57

World Geography Puzzles Australia and Oceania

Name: _____ Date: _____

Australia and Oceania: Locations of Major Cities

Directions: Location is the position of a place on Earth's surface. The absolute location is the latitude and longitude coordinates of a place. Find and circle the cities listed below in the word search puzzle. Words can go horizontally, vertically, and diagonally in all eight directions. Then using an atlas or the Internet, find the latitude and longitude coordinates of the cities, and list them on your own paper. Coordinates may vary slightly from atlas to atlas.

```
K F Z H L A D A M S T O W N B L T R N M M D J C R C R L
V K N X T R X R Z R Y K M R V D B B V P N H T L L T A G
X M Q T O R G K G T G M I N H A M M L A N M G T A L G Z
N T Q R L F E M N N L S Y O J L J V L L J R K R C Q A Z
B C O W N F C P M F B M R T F A M K M A L M A X J X N K
K K F L P Y O T N A X L B G X P C D A R L W N I W R A D
M K Z Y V R T P N N M F X N Z U S T D R A R N T K Y O D
T R Y Y T Q N E N T B K V I A L G L E E M N W Z P G W K
M V F V B K N R H M X H L L R I N G L B L N H K A J N L
Z R I O H S X Z A O X P W L P G I X A N D K E P K M G T
G L D G N P E T B G B K M E N A R B I A X G O R Q K V V
A N X U C G A R M Y L A N W O D P C D C F G K M A X J V
K J T R N U A G O H P P R Y U A S F E T A Z Y G T Y K J
P J F L T E N F M M T A E T M R E K Q P V X K Y X V A M
T W N U G Z D P A W T N P D E R C X P R R G Y F P P W N
N G A Z N M R I R L D R T E A I I M E L B O U R N E E A
L H G I M G L R N Y E B O M E T L Y H P Z N Q G P T W P
Z H K T P L D K S P V Q M P B T A T K F A R A I N O H I
Q S U V A A R I K I L A P T B P E M D T K V F C Z Y K A
V A F O L A U K U N L H C H R I S T C H U R C H W L L S
```

1. ADAMSTOWN
2. ADELAIDE
3. AGANA
4. ALICE SPRINGS
5. APIA
6. AUCKLAND
7. BRISBANE
8. CANBERRA
9. CHRISTCHURCH
10. DALAP-ULIGA-DARRIT
11. DARWIN
12. DUNEDIN
13. FONGAFALE
14. HOBART
15. HONIARA
16. KOROR
17. MATA-UTU
18. MELBOURNE
19. NOUMEA
20. NUKU'ALOFA
21. PAGO PAGO
22. PALIKIR
23. PAPEETE
24. PERTH
25. PORT MORESBY
26. PORT VILA
27. SAIPAN
28. SUVA
29. SYDNEY
30. TARAWA
31. WELLINGTON
32. WEWAK
33. YAREN

World Geography Puzzles   Australia and Oceania

Name: _____ Date: _____

Australia and Oceania: Physical Features

Directions: Use the clues below and an atlas or the Internet to help you complete the crossword puzzle about the physical features of Australia and Oceania.

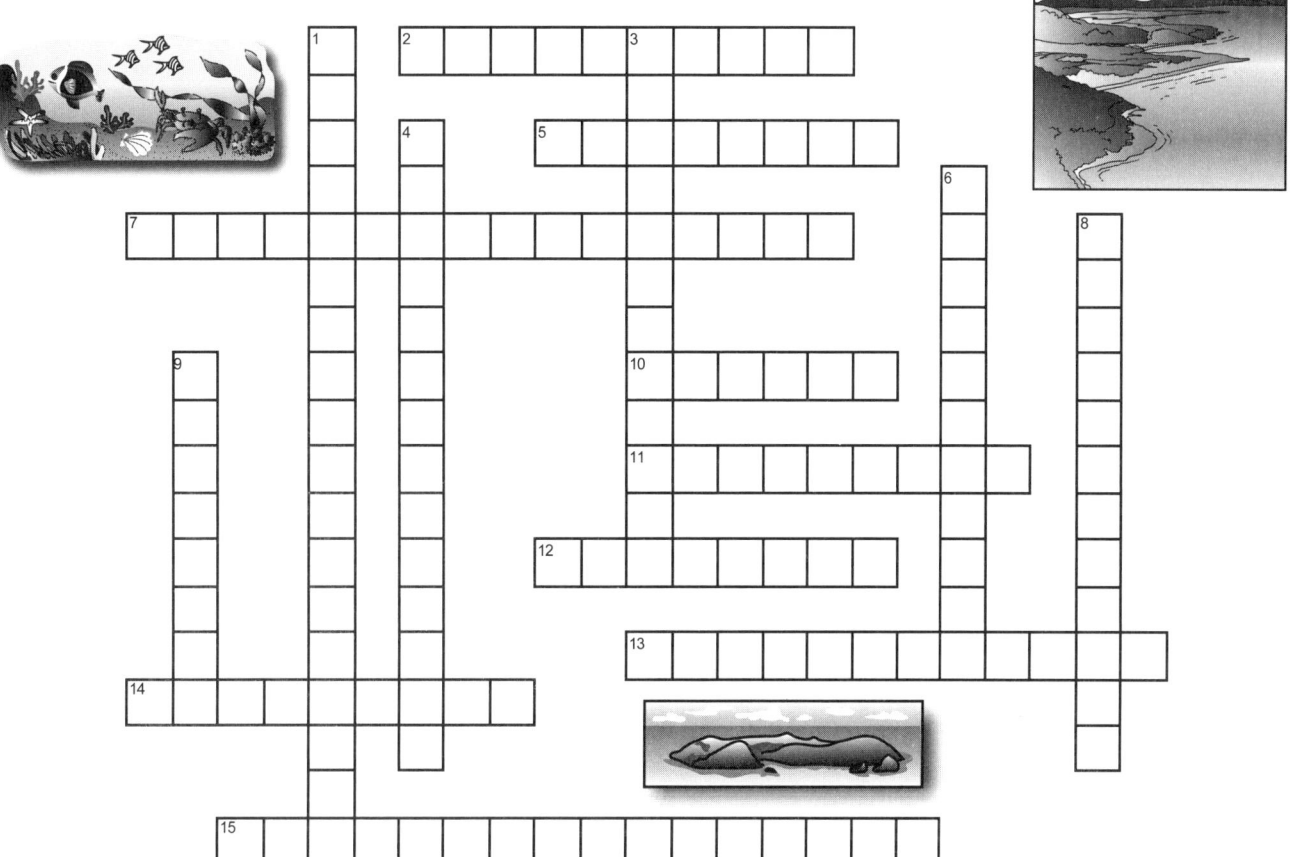

ACROSS

2. Body of water separating New Zealand's North and South Islands (two words)
5. Body of water between Australia and the Solomon Islands (two words)
7. One of the deserts in the outback of Western Australia (three words)
10. This is the major island in French Polynesia.
11. Landmark rock formation located in Australia's outback (two words)
12. Famous as the island where mutineers from the HMS *Bounty* settled in 1790
13. Papua New Guinea's highest mountain at 14,880 feet (4,510 meters) (two words)
14. The two major islands of Fiji are ____ ____ and Viti Levu.
15. Coral makes up this large natural formation off the northeast coast of Australia. (three words)

DOWN

1. Mountains along the eastern coast of Australia (three words)
3. Body of water between Australia's Cape York Peninsula and Papua New Guinea (two words)
4. This part of the Mariana Ocean Trench is the deepest point on Earth at 35,840 feet (10,924 meters) below sea level. (two words)
6. This island, which is one of the Solomon Islands, was the site of an air and sea battle between the United States and Japan during World War II.
8. Mountains on New Zealand's South Island (two words)
9. Island separated from Australia by the Bass Strait

CD-404133 © Mark Twain Media, Inc., Publishers   59

World Geography Puzzles Australia and Oceania

Name: _____ Date: _____

Australia and Oceania: Plants, Animals, and Resources

Directions: Use the clues below to help you unscramble the names of plants, animals, resources, and industries that are found in Australia and Oceania.

1. This dried coconut meat that yields coconut oil is an export of many islands, such as Kiribati, Palau, Tuvalu, and Vanuatu. RCPAO _____

2. Many members of this mammal family that carry their young in a pouch are only found in Australia. UAIASRPLM _____

3. This Australian tree is harvested for timber and to make fiberboard and paper products. Oil is also distilled from the leaves. It is the main diet of koalas. UELACTSYUP _____

4. New Caledonia has rich deposits of this metal. KLINEC _____

5. On many of the islands of Oceania and along the coast of Australia, this is a major industry. HFINSIG _____

6. This highly scented species of acacia is the national flower of Australia. GDOELN WTLATE _____

7. New Zealand's _____ industry produces sheep, beef and dairy cattle, barley, wheat, fruits, and potatoes. GCILEUTARRU _____

8. This Australian bird is about the size of a crow and has a call that sounds like loud laughter. RKBUROAAKO _____

9. These gems are one of Australia's exports. LAPOS _____

10. Australia is the world's largest producer of this textile material. LOWO _____

11. This small flightless bird of New Zealand is also the nickname for a person from New Zealand. IWKI _____

12. This is one of two egg-laying mammals that is only found in Australia. UPLSAYPT _____

13. Papua New Guinea exports minerals such as _____ and gold. OPRCEP _____

14. Some of the island nations of Oceania, such as Fiji and French Polynesia, are popular _____ destinations. ROTTISU _____

15. There are about 50 species of this hopping, pouched mammal in Australia. AOKRGAON _____

Australia and Oceania: Movement of Early People and Culture

The continent of Australia and the islands of Oceania were isolated from Asia and the western world for much of their history. While there was travel between islands, the difficulty of crossing the ocean led most natives to settle on a specific island or group of islands. This allowed unique cultures to develop in the Pacific region that were not seen in other places. These cultures include the Aborigines in Australia, the Polynesians on many of the Pacific islands, and the Maori in New Zealand.

It is believed that the Aborigines crossed over land bridges from Asia to Australia at a time when the earth's oceans were lower, possibly as long ago as 40,000 years. After the sea level rose and covered these land bridges, migration was cut off. The Aborigines were hunter-gatherers. They did not raise animals for food. They used dingoes, the wild dogs of Australia, to help them hunt. Their weapons included spears, clubs, and boomerangs. When thrown correctly, a curved wooden boomerang will fly away from the thrower, hit the intended prey, and return to the thrower.

More than 500 tribes of Aborigines lived on the continent at one time. At their peak, there may have been as many as 750,000 in Australia and its neighboring islands. However, as Europeans explored and settled the land, they brought diseases for which the Aborigines had no resistance. They were also driven out of their traditional territories. Many were killed due to racial violence or died from malnutrition. By 1965, only about 40,000 Aborigines of pure descent were left. Today, those claiming to have some Aboriginal heritage number about 500,000 or 2.5 percent of Australia's population. Recently, the government has reversed its policies and is now working to help protect the Aborigines and restore their rights.

DNA evidence suggests that Polynesians are descended from the people of southeast Asia. It is believed they started out in Taiwan and spread through the islands of southeast Asia. From there, they moved west into the islands of the Pacific, including Melanesia, Fiji, Samoa, the Cook Islands, Marquesas, Hawaii, Tahiti, Pitcairn, Tonga, and New Zealand. They traveled in large ocean-going migration canoes.

By about A.D. 1280, the Polynesians had settled many of the Pacific islands and had made it to New Zealand. The culture that developed in New Zealand was called the Maori. The word means "natural" or "ordinary" in the native language. The first Maori to settle in New Zealand were hunters, especially of the many large birds of the islands. Eventually, they developed farming skills and began to grow crops. However, competition for resources led to an increase in warfare among the tribes, and the Maori became known as a fierce people.

Australia and Oceania: Movement of Early People and Culture (cont.)

In the early 1600s, European sailing vessels began to encounter the islands of the Pacific and the shores of Australia as they were blown off course on their way to trade in the Moluccas or the Philippines. The Dutch explorer Abel Tasman sailed south of Australia and first encountered Tasmania and New Zealand in 1642–43. The Englishman James Cook was the most well-known of the explorers of the region. He made three voyages to the Pacific in 1768–71, 1772–75, and 1776–80.

Eventually, European colonization and inter-tribal warfare led to a decrease in the Maori population. The British annexed New Zealand in 1840, and the Maori became British subjects. By the 1890s, the Maori had lost 95 percent of their land. The Maori population declined from about 100,000 in 1840 to about 42,000 in 1896. However, during the twentieth century, the Maori culture went through a revival. Maori politicians were able to secure civil rights and restoration of lands for their people. There are seven designated Maori seats in Parliament. Most Maori people have intermarried with Europeans or other immigrants and now live in cities and towns, but there is a strong movement to preserve their language, arts, crafts, and culture.

Directions: Choose from the words listed below that have to do with the native people and cultures of Australia and Oceania to fill in the puzzle on page 63. Use the letters provided and the length of the word to help you find the correct words that fit in the puzzle. Not all the words will be used. The first one is done for you.

Abel Tasman	disease	land bridge	population
Aborigines	DNA evidence	language	revival
annexed	Dutch	malnutrition	Samoa
Australia	Europeans	Maori	southeast Asia
boomerang	farming	migration	Tahiti
British	fierce	natural	Taiwan
canoes	gatherers	New Zealand	Tonga
civil rights	Hawaii	ordinary	voyage
colonization	hunters	Pacific	warfare
competition	islands	Parliament	
culture	isolated	politicians	
dingoes	James Cook	Polynesians	

World Geography Puzzles
Australia and Oceania

Name: _____ Date: _____

Australia and Oceania: Movement of Early People and Culture (cont.)

Directions: Complete the puzzle with words from the list on page 62. Use the letters provided and the length of the word to help you find the correct words that fit in the puzzle. Not all the words will be used. The first one is done for you.

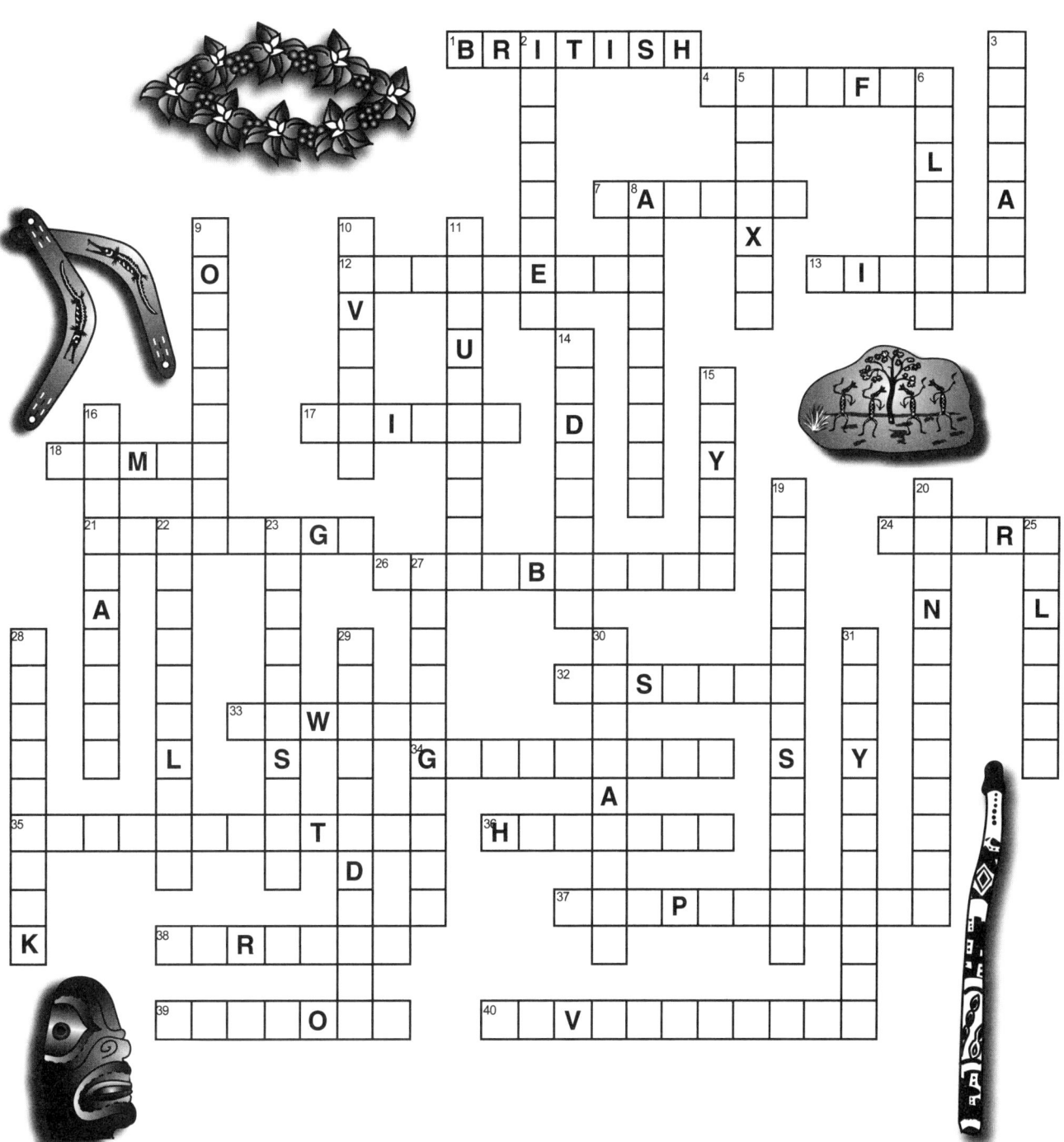

World Geography Puzzles Australia and Oceania

Name: _____ Date: _____

Australia and Oceania: Regions

Directions: The islands of the western and central South Pacific Ocean are divided into regions called Micronesia, Melanesia, and Polynesia. Australia, New Zealand, and Papua New Guinea are also considered part of Oceania. Using an atlas, the Internet, or other reference sources, research the islands and countries below. Then place them in the correct category in the graphic organizer.

American Samoa   Australia   Bismarck Archipelago (Papua New Guinea)
Cook Islands   Federated States of Micronesia Fiji
French Polynesia   Gilbert Islands (Kiribati)   Guam
Hawaiian Islands (USA) Marshall Islands   Nauru
New Caledonia   New Zealand   Niue   Northern Mariana Islands
Palau   Papua New Guinea   Phoenix Islands (Kiribati)
Pitcairn Islands   Solomon Islands   Tonga
Tuvalu   Vanuatu   Western Samoa

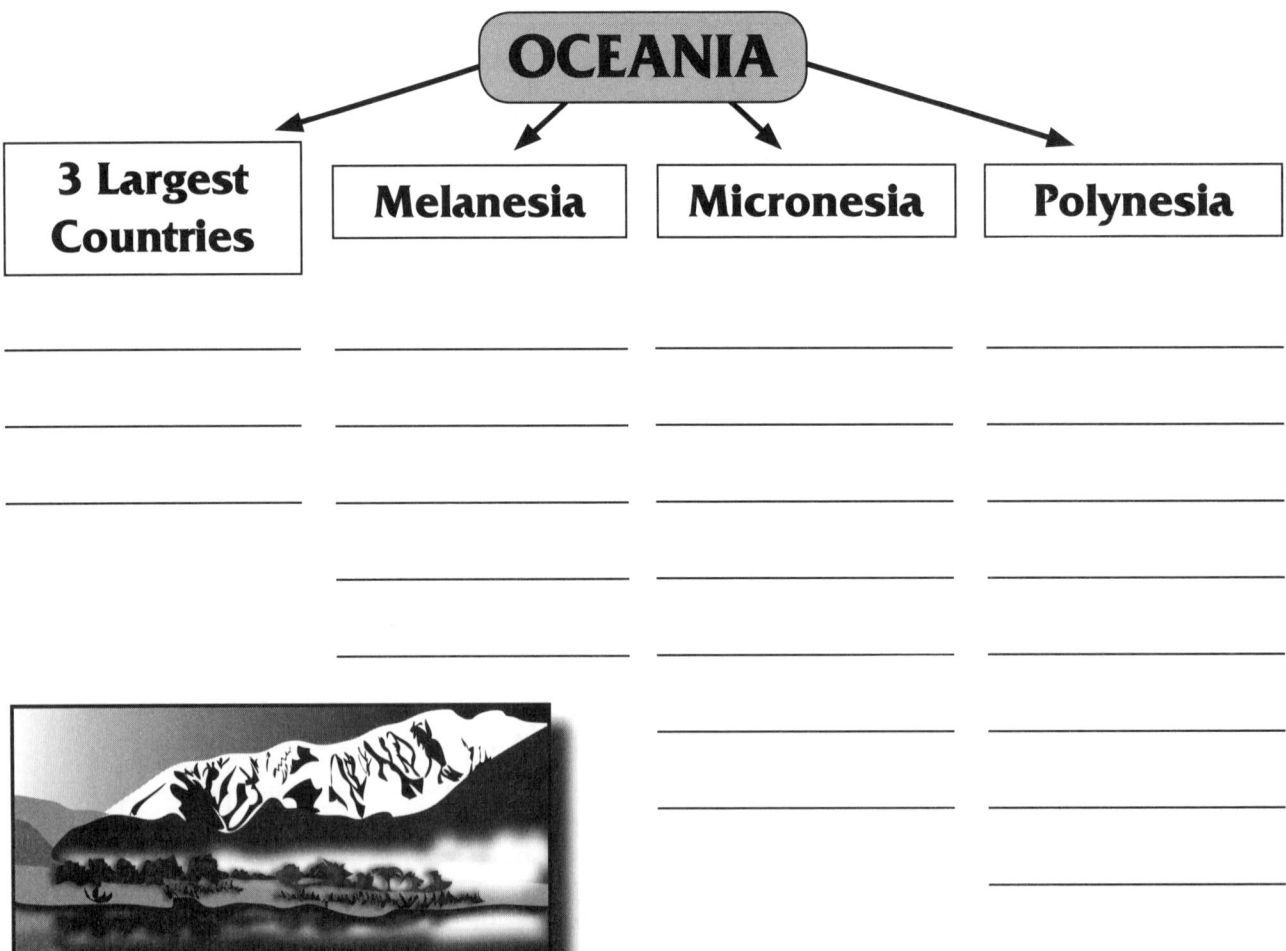

World Geography Puzzles Antarctica

Name: _____ Date: _____

Antarctica: Location

Directions: Location is the position of a place on Earth's surface. The absolute location is the latitude and longitude coordinates of a place. Find and circle the places and geographical features listed below in the word search puzzle. Words can go horizontally, vertically, and diagonally in all eight directions. Then using an atlas or the Internet, find the latitude and longitude coordinates of the places, and list them on your own paper. Some of these features cover a wide area, so you may have to give a range of latitude and longitude for the location. Coordinates may vary slightly from atlas to atlas.

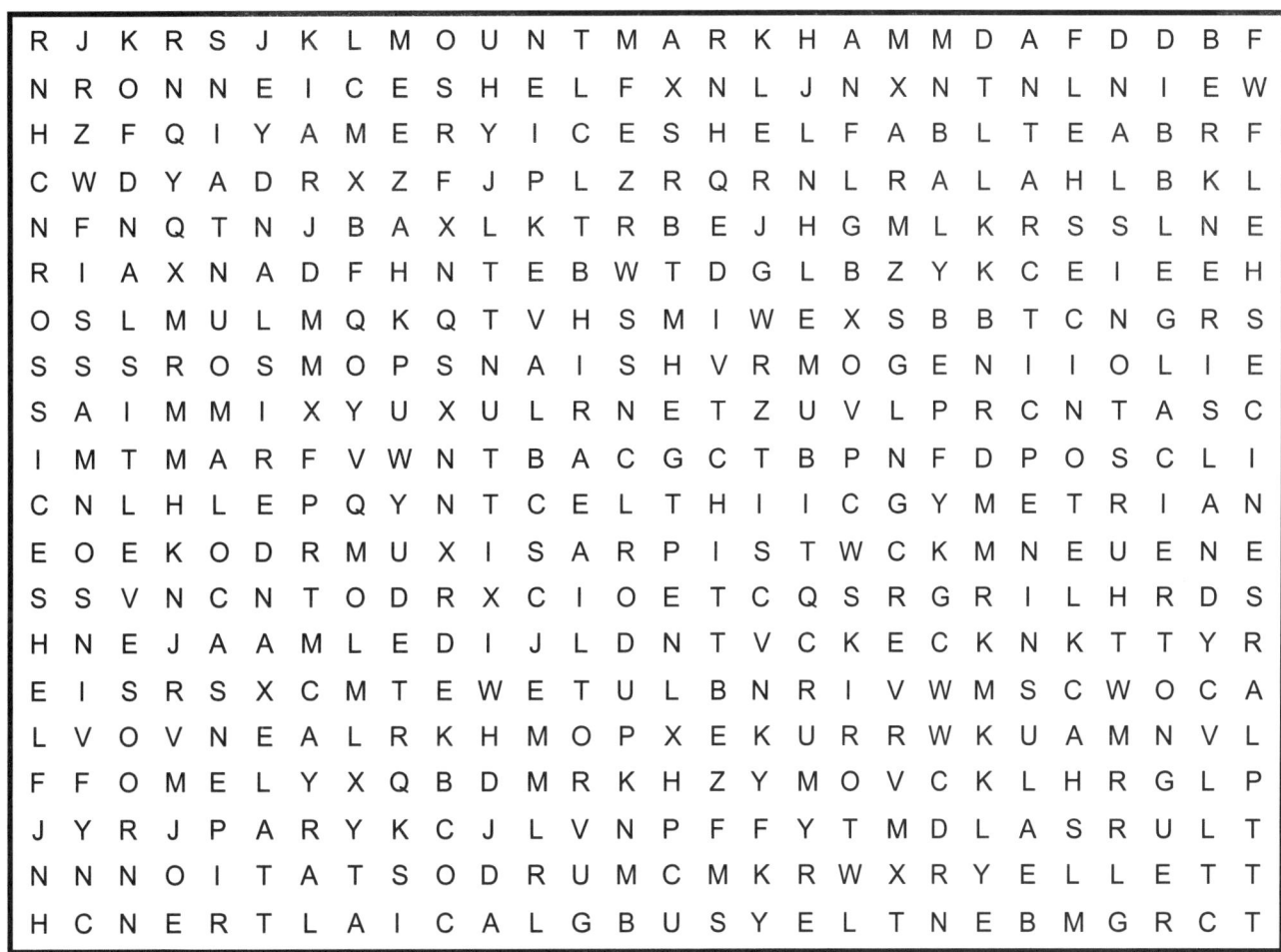

1. ALEXANDER ISLAND
2. AMERICAN HIGHLAND
3. AMERY ICE SHELF
4. ANTARCTIC CIRCLE
5. ANTARCTIC PENINSULA
6. BENTLEY SUBGLACIAL TRENCH
7. BERKNER ISLAND
8. DIBBLE GLACIER TONGUE
9. LAMBERT GLACIER
10. LARSEN ICE SHELF
11. McMURDO STATION
12. MOUNT EREBUS
13. MOUNT LISTER
14. MOUNT MARKHAM
15. MOUNT SIDLEY
16. MOUNT SIPLE
17. PENSACOLA MOUNTAINS
18. RONNE ICE SHELF
19. ROOSEVELT ISLAND
20. ROSS ICE SHELF
21. SHACKLETON ICE SHELF
22. SOUTH POLE
23. THURSTON ISLAND
24. VINSON MASSIF
25. WEST ICE SHELF

World Geography Puzzles

Antarctica

Name: _____ Date: _____

Antarctica: Physical Features

Directions: Use the clues below and an atlas or the Internet to help you complete the crossword puzzle about the physical features of Antarctica.

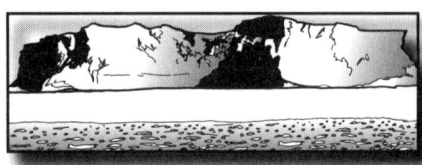

ACROSS

2. Ice-free areas of Antarctica where no rain has fallen for all of recorded history; Extremely dry winds cause any snow blown here to evaporate before hitting the ground. (two words)
5. The seas surrounding Antarctica where the Atlantic, Pacific, and Indian Oceans meet; also called the Southern Ocean (two words)
9. Mountains that divide the continent into West Antarctica and East Antarctica (two words)
11. Seawater ice that forms a 300–1,800 mile (483–2,897 km) wide belt around Antarctica in the winter (two words)
13. This forms as Lambert Glacier flows out over the ocean. (three words)
14. Tallest mountain in Antarctica (two words)
15. A river of ice that moves down a valley to the sea; One example is the Lambert.

DOWN

1. Its location varies as the earth's magnetic field changes. It is currently off the coast of Antarctica near 64°S, 138°E (three words)
3. Narrow arm of land that sticks out from the continent between 60° and 80°W longitude (two words)
4. Island surrounded by the Ronne and Filchner Ice Shelves (two words)
6. Body of water along Antarctica's coast at 180° longitude (two words)
7. Line of latitude at about 66°33"S; South of this line, there are 24 hours of daylight in midsummer and 24 hours of darkness in midwinter. (two words)
8. A mountain peak protruding out of the surrounding glacial ice; Vinson Massif is an example.
10. Place where a huge ice sheet has moved past the coastline out over the water and is floating; An example is the Ronne. (two words)
12. The process in which huge chunks of ice break off ice sheets, shelves, or glaciers to form icebergs

CD-404133 © Mark Twain Media, Inc., Publishers

World Geography Puzzles   Antarctica

Name: _____ Date: _____

Antarctica: Plants and Animals

Directions: Using the code key below, decode the missing words in the paragraphs.

    Antarctica's dry and bitterly cold __ __ __ __ __ __ __ limits its plant and animal
                                                 4 21 9 12 11 23 24
life. Most of the plant life are single-celled __ __ __ __ __ __ __ __ __. Algae,
                                                    1 13 5 11 8 9 7 12 7
__ __ __ __ __ __ __ __, fungi, lichens, and mosses grow on the few land outcroppings.
22 11 4 23 24 13 9 11
Only two flowering plants, __ __ __ __ __ __ __ __ __ and a flowering grass, grow south
                               20 24 11 13 21 14 1 13 23
of 60°S latitude. __ __ __ __ __ __ __ grows in most of the continent's coastal waters.
                 7 24 11 14 24 24 19
    __ __ __ __ __ is the most important animal in Antarctica. It is a small shrimp-like
     15 13 9 21 21
animal in the ocean that grows to about 1.5 inch (4 cm) long. Antarctica's __ __ __ __,
                                                                               10 9 7 18
birds, seals, and whales all feed on krill.

    Forty species of seabirds, including seven species of __ __ __ __ __ __ __ __,
                                                                    20 24 8 5 2 9 8 7
live on Antarctica for at least part of the year. The __ __ __ __ __ __ __ penguin is the
                                                             24 12 20 24 13 1 13
only species that spends all year on the sea ice attached to the continent. The
__ __ __ __ __ __ __ __ __ is another seabird that lives on the continent.
11 21 22 11 23 13 1 7 7
The __ __ __ __ __ __ __ __ __ __ raises its young in the Arctic but
      11 13 4 23 9 4 23 24 13 8
spends the rest of the year in Antarctica. Other birds include the snow petrel, the blue-eyed
__ __ __ __ __ __ __ __ __, the Dominican gull, and the brown skua.
4 1 13 12 1 13 11 8 23

    Five species of true seals live in the region. These are the Weddell, Ross,
__ __ __ __ __ __ __, crabeater, and elephant seals. The __ __ __ __ __ __
21 24 1 20 11 13 19   14 24 19 19 24 21 21
seal is the only one that lives all year on or under the ice attached to the continent.
The southern __ __ __ __ __ __ __ is also found in Antarctica.
                10 2 13 7 24 11 21
    Several kinds of __ __ __ __ __ __ whales spend at least
                      22 11 21 24 24 8
part of the year in Antarctica's waters. These include the blue, fin, sei, minke,
__ __ __ __ __ __ __ __, and southern right whales. These whales filter krill from the
18 2 12 20 22 11 4 15
water. The sperm whale and the __ __ __ __ __ __ whale are two types of toothed whales
                                        15 9 21 21 24 13
that feed in Antarctica's waters. Killer whales, also called __ __ __ __, hunt the seals that
                                                                              1 13 4 11
live on the continent's coasts.
    Eight species of __ __ __ __ __ __ __ are also found in the waters off Antarctica.
                       19 1 21 20 18 9 8

A	B	C	D	E	F	G	H	I	J	K	L	M	N	O	P	Q	R	S	T	U	V	W	X	Y	Z
11	22	4	19	24	10	5	18	9	3	15	21	12	8	1	20	16	13	7	23	2	25	14	6	26	17

Antarctica: Exploration

Directions: Use the clues below and an atlas or the Internet to unscramble the words associated with the early exploration of Antarctica.

1. This Greek philosopher believed there must be a huge land in the Southern Hemisphere to balance the known land in the north. He named it *Antarktikos*, which means "opposite the arctic."

   IASRTOETL
   _____

2. Egyptian geographer Ptolemy had this name for the southern continent, which means "southern, unknown land."

   ARTER LIAARSTSU ITAIGONCN
   _____
   _____

3. In 1773, this British captain crossed the Antarctic Circle and saw many icebergs but did not get close enough to see Antarctica.

   ASMEJ OCOK
   _____

4. Fabian Gottlieb von _____ from Russia was the first to see the mainland of Antarctica in 1819 and 1820.

   ALNEENGSBHSLIU
   _____

5. American captain _____ _____ was the first person to set foot on Antarctica.

   HJNO IDVSA
   _____

6. The _____ _____ and a type of seal are named for British sailor James Weddell.

   DLDEELW EAS
   _____

7. James Clark Ross discovered the huge _____ _____ that was named for him.

   CEI FELHS
   _____

8. Between 1901 and 1904, Robert Falcon Scott and his men spent two winters in McMurdo Sound and made the first attempt to reach the _____ _____.

   SUHTO LEPO
   _____

9. Norwegian Roald _____ and his men were the first to reach the South Pole on December 14, 1911.

   MDESUANN
   _____

10. Ernest _____ and his men spent over a year on the ice in 1914–1915 when their ship was trapped by ice and later sank.

    OHNTKALECS
    _____

Antarctica: International Agreements and Possible Resources

Antarctica has been set aside as a place for nonmilitary, nonpolitical research. July 1, 1957, through December 31, 1958, was declared the International Geophysical Year (IGY). A major multinational research effort occurred throughout that year's time, with an emphasis on research in Antarctica.

Although many nations had made claims to territory in Antarctica, 12 governments signed the Antarctic Treaty on December 1, 1959. This provided for peaceful use of Antarctica for scientific investigation. No nuclear explosions or nuclear waste disposal would be allowed. The nations did not have to give up their claims, and no new claims could be made.

Today, research continues in about 50 stations maintained by various nations. About 3,500 researchers are on the continent in the summer, and about 1,000 remain through the winter months, but there is no permanent population. In addition, thousands of tourists visit the continent by cruise ship or for extreme expeditions.

Since the geology of Antarctica is similar to mineral-rich regions of South America, South Africa, and Australia, it is believed that a wide variety of minerals are located in Antarctica. These could include platinum, antimony, chromium, copper, gold, lead, molybdenum, tin, uranium, zinc, diamonds, oil, and natural gas. The only substantial mineral deposits found so far are coal in the Transantarctic Mountains and iron ore near the Prince Charles Mountains of East Antarctica. However, due to the difficulty of exploring for minerals and the extremely high cost to mine and transport them, no mining has been done.

Because Antarctica's continental ice sheet contains about 90% of the world's glacial ice, this could be a huge source of freshwater. But again, the cost of harvesting and delivering the ice is too high to make it practical. It has also been suggested that Antarctica could be a long-term storage site for grain and other food. This will also have to wait until cost-effective ways to build storage facilities and transport and handle the food are developed.

As long as cheaper alternatives can be found elsewhere, it is unlikely that Antarctica's resources will be developed.

World Geography Puzzles
Antarctica

Name: _____ Date: _____

Antarctica: International Agreements and Possible Resources (cont.)

Directions: Choose from the words listed below that have to do with the nations involved in Antarctica and the resources that may be present on the continent. Use the letters provided and the length of the word to help you find the correct words that fit in the puzzle. The first one is done for you.

Argentina	United Kingdom	iron ore
Australia	United States	lead
Belgium	antimony	molybdenum
Chile	chromium	natural gas
France	coal	oil
Japan	copper	platinum
New Zealand	diamonds	storage
Norway	freshwater	tin
South Africa	gold	uranium
Soviet Union	ice	zinc

Answer Keys

Maps: Crossword (p. 3)

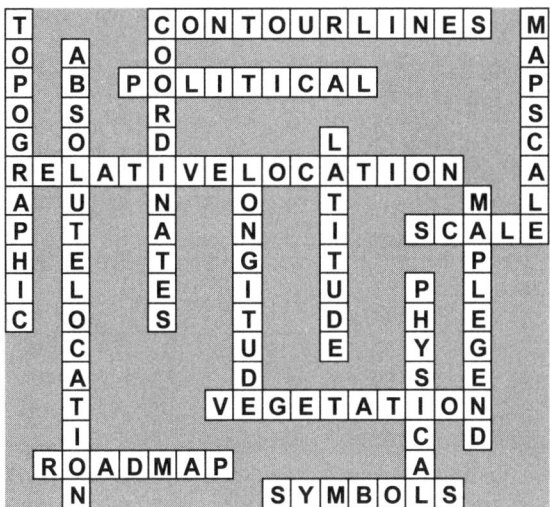

Latitude and Longitude: Word Search (p. 5)

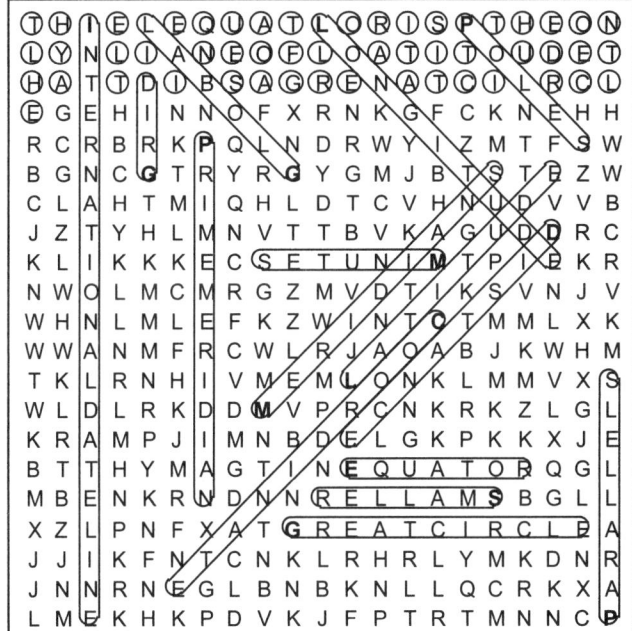

1. coordinate
2. distance
3. equator
4. Global
5. great circle
6. grid
7. International Date Line
8. Latitude
9. Longitude
10. meridians
11. minutes
12. parallels
13. Poles
14. Prime Meridian
15. smaller

Hidden Message: The equator is the only line of latitude that is a great circle.

Earth's Hemispheres and Continents: Matching (p. 7)

1. E, W, N, S
2. E, W, N, S
3. W, N
4. E, S
5. W, N, S
6. E, W, S
7. E, W, N
8. W, S
9. E, N
10. E, N
11. W, N
12. E, S
13. W, N
14. E, N
15. E, N, S
16. E, N
17. W, S
18. W, N
19. E, W, N
20. E, N
21. W, N, S
22. E, N, S
23. E, N
24. W, N
25. W, S
26. E, N, S
27. W, N
28. E, W, N
29. W, N, S
30. E, N
31. E, W, N
32. E, N
33. E, N
34. W, N
35. W, S
36. E, N
37. W, N
38. E, N, S
39. W, N
40. E, S

Earth's Seasons: Decoding (p. 9)

1. equator
2. hemispheres
3. spring
4. vernal equinox
5. Summer
6. solstice
7. autumnal
8. December
9. winter
10. revolves
11. tilted
12. ellipse
13. sunlight
14. directly
15. season

Day and Night on Earth: Word Search (p. 11)

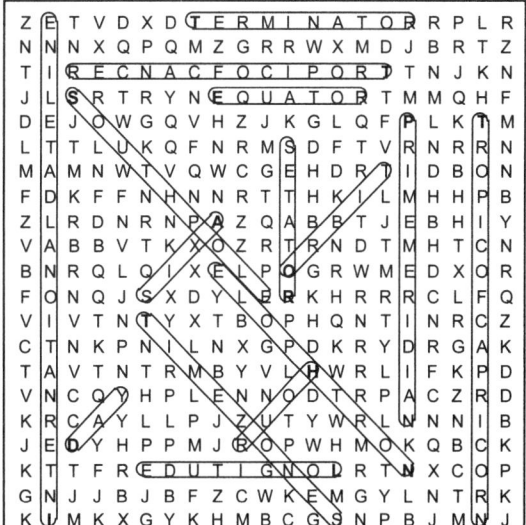

1. axis
2. day
3. equator
4. hour
5. International Date Line
6. longitude
7. North Pole
8. orbit
9. Prime Meridian
10. rotates
11. South Pole
12. terminator
13. time zones
14. Tropic of Cancer
15. Tropic of Capricorn

World Geography Puzzles — Answer Keys

Earth's Wind Belts: Crossword Puzzle (p. 13)

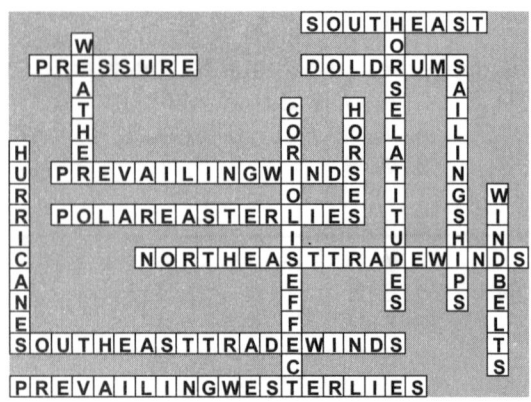

Ocean Currents: Hidden Message (p. 15)
1. CURRENTS
2. GRAND BANKS
3. CALIFORNIA
4. NORTH EQUATORIAL
5. PERU
6. WATER VAPOR
7. CANARY
8. WARM CURRENT
9. GULF STREAM
10. COLD CURRENT
11. CIRCULAR
12. NORTH ATLANTIC DRIFT

Hidden Message: EL NINO CURRENT

Cultures From Around the World: Word Scramble (p. 17)
1. IMMIGRANTS
2. CULTURE
3. LANGUAGE
4. CELEBRATION
5. CUSTOMS
6. COVERINGS
7. GERMAN
8. IRELAND
9. SWEET POTATOES
10. NATIVE AMERICAN
11. THANKSGIVING
12. CLOTHES
13. CHINESE
14. COMMUNITY
15. WEDDING

Location: Word Search (p. 19)

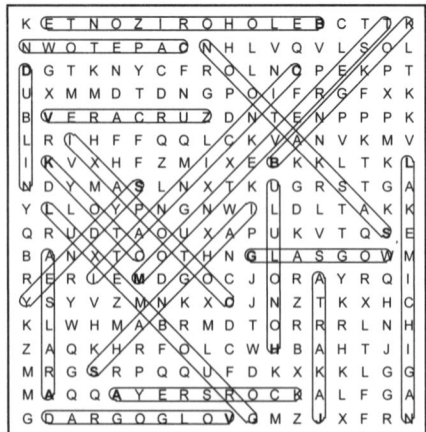

These coordinates are approximate. Accept reasonable answers.
1. 21°N, 158°W
2. 28°N, 87°E
3. 56°N, 4°W
4. 35°N, 136°E
5. 44°N, 87°W
6. 34°S, 151°E
7. 34°S, 18°E
8. 52°N, 107°W
9. 45°N, 60°E
10. 14°N, 100°E
11. 19°N, 96°W
12. 50°N, 6°E
13. 53°N, 6°W
14. 20°S, 44°W
15. 39°N, 84°W
16. 0°, 78°W
17. 49°N, 44°E
18. 6°S, 107°E
19. 31°N, 121°E
20. 28°S, 131°E

Place: Describe It (p. 21)
Answers will vary.

Human-Environment Interaction: Crossword Puzzle (p. 23)

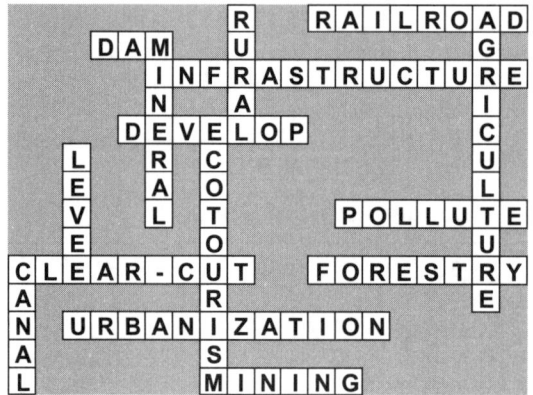

Movement: Decoding (p. 25)
1. People
2. Movement
3. communication
4. agriculture
5. manufacturing
6. languages
7. World Wide Web
8. Raw materials
9. infrastructure
10. river

Regions: Word Search (p. 27)

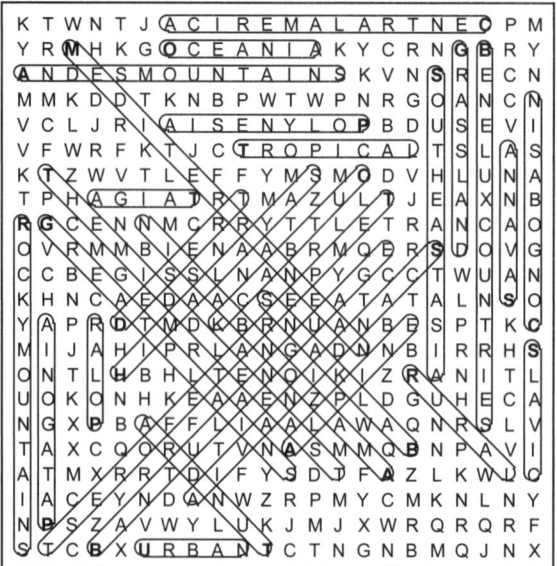

World Geography Puzzles — Answer Keys

North America: Locations of Major Cities (p. 28)

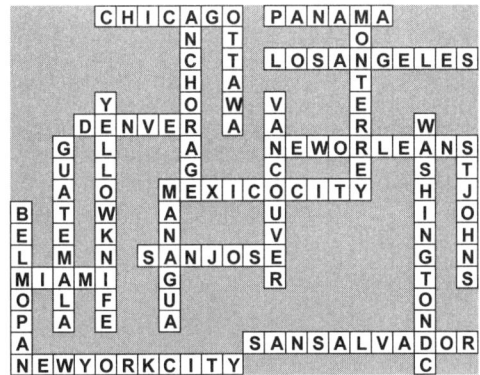

North America: Physical Features (p. 29)

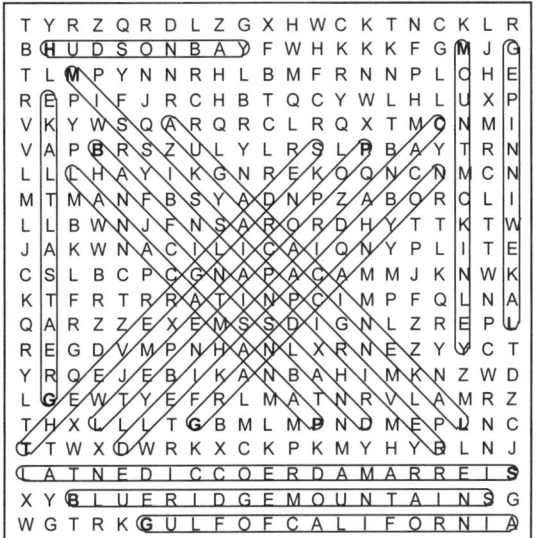

1. Utah, USA
2. Mexico
3. Florida, USA
4. Canada
5. United States
6. Alaska, USA
7. Mexico
8. Panama
9. Manitoba, Canada
10. United States
11. Canada
12. Nicaragua
13. Mexico
14. Arizona, USA
15. Canada

North America: Plants, Animals, and Resources (p. 30)

petroleum
silver
California
Canada
exports
crude
antelope
bison
jaguar
polar

coal
Agriculture
vegetables
Fishing
machinery
coffee
gophers
caribou
grizzly
Whales

cottonmouth
beaded
finfish
hummingbird
herons
tropical
falcons

copperhead
freshwater
sharks
condor
pelicans
prey

North America: Native Americans (p. 32)

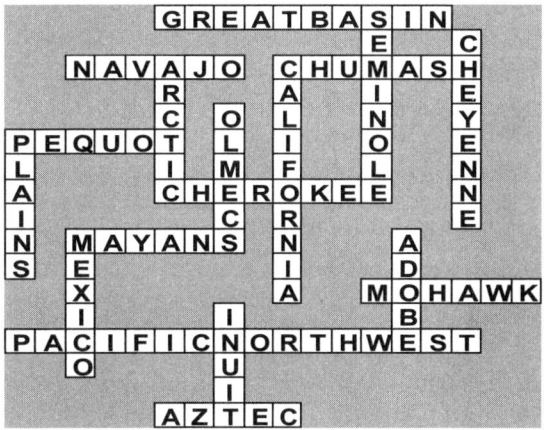

North America: Regions (p. 33)

1. NEW ENGLAND
2. MEDITERRANEAN
3. GREAT PLAINS
4. TROPICAL RAINFOREST
5. RUST BELT
6. TUNDRA
7. RIVIERA
8. GREAT BASIN
9. CARIBBEAN
10. SUN BELT
11. HUMID CONTINENTAL
12. MARITIMES

South America: Locations of Major Cities (p. 34)

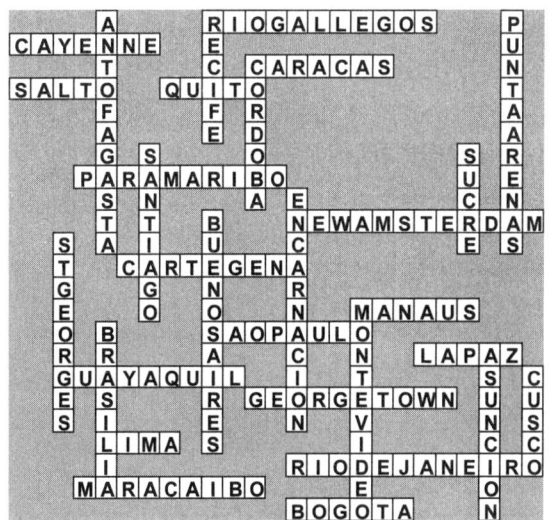

World Geography Puzzles — Answer Keys

South America: Physical Features (p. 35)
1. AND**E**S
2. CA**P**E HORN
3. MA**R**ACAIBO
4. **A**NGEL FALLS
5. ACONCAGUA
6. TITICA**C**A
7. AMAZ**O**N
8. ATACAM**A**
9. A**L**TIPLANO
10. R**I**O DE LA PLATA
11. **H**UASCARAN
12. STRAIT OF MA**G**ELLAN

Hidden Word: ARCHIPELAGO de los Chonos

South America: Plants, Animals, and Resources (p. 36)

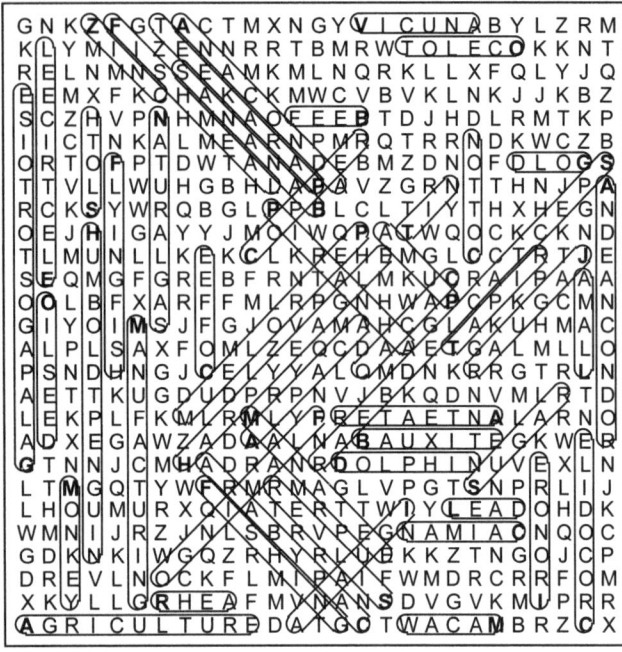

South America: Colonial Settlement (p. 38)
1. FRENCH GUIANA
2. BRAZIL
3. AFRICA
4. LAND BRIDGE
5. ENGLISH
6. WATERWAYS
7. BUENOS AIRES
8. CONQUISTADORS
9. INCA
10. ANDES MOUNTAINS
11. MESTIZOS
12. DUTCH

South America: Regions (p. 39)

Europe: Locations of Major Cities (p. 40)

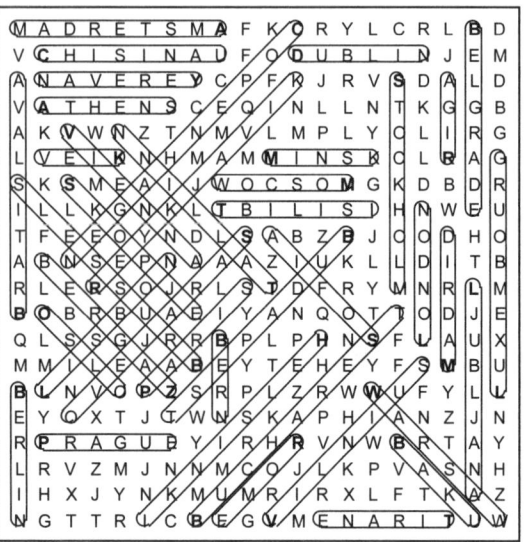

These coordinates are approximate.
Accept reasonable answers.

1. 52°N, 5°E
2. 38°N, 24°E
3. 40°N, 50°E
4. 45°N, 21°E
5. 52°N, 13°E
6. 47°N, 7°E
7. 48°N, 17°E
8. 51°N, 4°E
9. 44°N, 26°E
10. 47°N, 19°E
11. 47°N, 29°E
12. 56°N, 12°E
13. 53°N, 6°W
14. 60°N, 25°E
15. 50°N, 31°E
16. 39°N, 9°W
17. 46°N, 14°E
18. 51°N, 0°
19. 50°N, 6°E
20. 40°N, 4°W
21. 54°N, 28°E
22. 56°N, 38°E
23. 60°N, 11°E
24. 49°N, 2°E
25. 50°N, 14°E
26. 64°N, 22°W
27. 57°N, 24°E
28. 42°N, 13°E
29. 43°N, 18°E
30. 42°N, 21°E
31. 43°N, 23°E
32. 59°N, 18°E
33. 59°N, 25°E
34. 42°N, 43°E
35. 41°N, 20°E
36. 48°N, 16°E
37. 55°N, 25°E
38. 52°N, 21°E
39. 40°N, 44°E
40. 46°N, 16°E

Europe: Physical Features (p. 41)
1. S
2. S
3. M
4. M
5. S
6. P
7. S
8. S
9. S
10. M
11. S
12. M
13. I
14. I
15. P
16. R
17. R
18. R
19. R
20. R
21. R
22. I
23. P
24. I
25. S
26. I
27. S
28. P
29. P
30. S
31. R
32. M
33. P
34. I
35. S
36. S
37. S
38. I
39. R
40. P
41. M
42. R
43. R
44. M
45. R
46. I
47. R
48. I
49. P
50. R
51. I
52. I
53. I
54. R
55. R
56. S
57. R
58. M
59. R
60. S

World Geography Puzzles — Answer Keys

Europe: Plants, Animals, and Resources (p. 42)

Agriculture	western	poultry
grains	olives	forestry
wood pulp	building	Cork
Denmark	mackerel	Salmon
caviar	Industrial	bauxite
nickel	natural gas	electronic
extinct	wolves	Chamois
Lapland	storks	

Europe: Movement of People, Goods, and Ideas (p. 44)

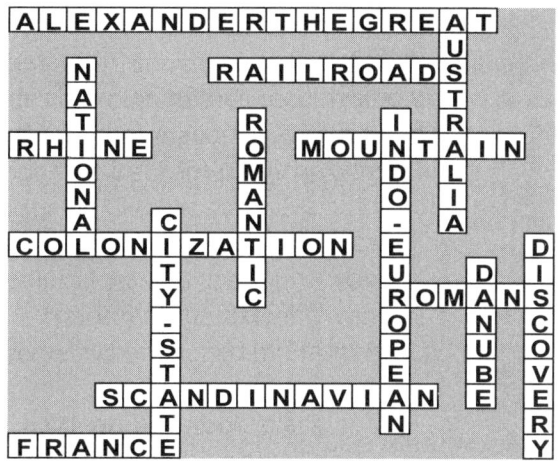

Europe: Regions (p. 45)

1. ALPINE
2. BALKANS
3. BAVARIA
4. MEDITERRANEAN
5. EUROPEAN UNION
6. CHAMPAGNE
7. BALTIC NATIONS
8. FRENCH RIVIERA
9. SCANDINAVIA
10. RHINE VALLEY
11. BRITISH ISLES
12. ANDALUSIA

Africa: Locations of Major Cities (p. 46)

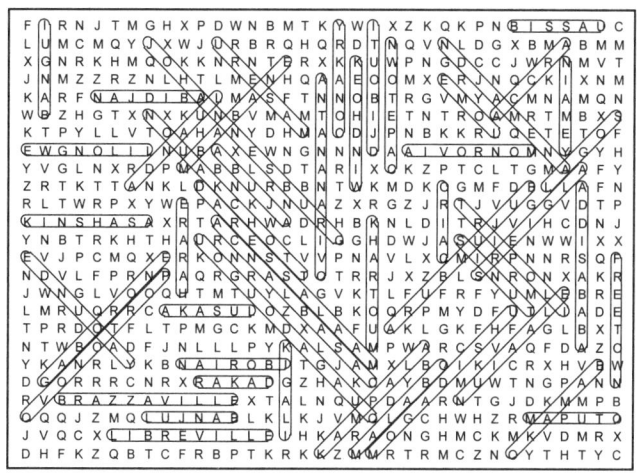

These coordinates are approximate. Accept reasonable answers.

1. 5°N, 4°W
2. 9°N, 7°E
3. 6°N, 0°
4. 9°N, 39°E
5. 37°N, 3°E
6. 19°S, 48°E
7. 13°N, 8°W
8. 4°N, 19°E
9. 13°N, 17°W
10. 12°N, 16°W
11. 4°S, 15°E
12. 3°S, 29°E
13. 30°N, 31°E
14. 34°S, 18°E
15. 34°N, 8°W
16. 9°N, 14°W
17. 15°N, 17°W
18. 7°S, 39°E
19. 12°N, 43°E
20. 27°N, 13°W
21. 8°N, 13°W
22. 25°S, 25°E
23. 18°S, 31°E
24. 26°S, 28°E
25. 0°, 33°E
26. 16°N, 33°E
27. 2°S, 30°E
28. 4°S, 15°E
29. 7°N, 3°E
30. 0°, 9°E
31. 14°S, 33°E
32. 6°N, 1°E
33. 9°S, 13°E
34. 15°S, 28°E
35. 4°N, 9°E
36. 26°S, 33°E
37. 29°S, 27°E
38. 26°S, 31°E
39. 2°N, 45°E
40. 6°N, 11°W
41. 1°S, 37°E
42. 12°N, 15°E
43. 14°N, 2°E
44. 18°N, 16°W
45. 12°N, 2°W
46. 7°N, 3°E
47. 33°N, 13°E
48. 37°N, 10°E
49. 22°S, 17°E
50. 4°N, 12°E

Africa: Physical Features (p. 47)

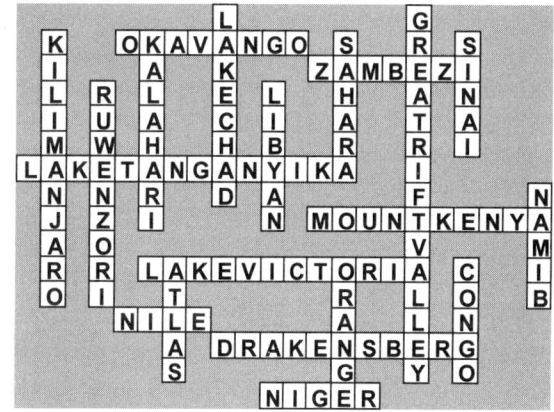

Africa: Plants, Animals, and Resources (p. 48)

1. URANIUM
2. MAHOGANY
3. YAMS
4. SHEEP
5. PETROLEUM
6. MICA
7. ANTELOPE
8. ELEPHANT
9. TITANIUM
10. MANUFACTURING
11. GOLD
12. DIAMONDS
13. SUBSISTENCE FARMING
14. GIRAFFE
15. EGRET
16. TEA
17. AARDVARK
18. KENAF
19. FENNEC
20. COBRA
21. ADDER
22. RHINOCEROS
23. SAND VIPER
24. RADIUM
25. MILLET
26. TENREC
27. CACAO
28. OSTRICH
29. HEDGEHOG
30. GORILLA
31. AGOUTI
32. IBIS
33. SALT
34. TOBACCO
35. OLIVE OIL
36. LION
37. NATURAL GAS

World Geography Puzzles — Answer Keys

Africa: Climate (p. 50)
1. TROPICAL SAVANNA
2. MEDITERRANEAN
3. SAHEL
4. PRECIPITATION
5. DESERTS
6. RAIN FOREST
7. DESERTIFICATION
8. STEPPE
9. GRASSLANDS
10. OCEAN CURRENTS

Africa: Regions of Conflict (p. 51)

independent	religious	international
displaced	Darfur	discriminating
Janjawid	Chad	Sudan
malnutrition	United Nations	Ethiopia
Eritrea	election	corrupt

Asia: Locations of Major Cities (p. 52)

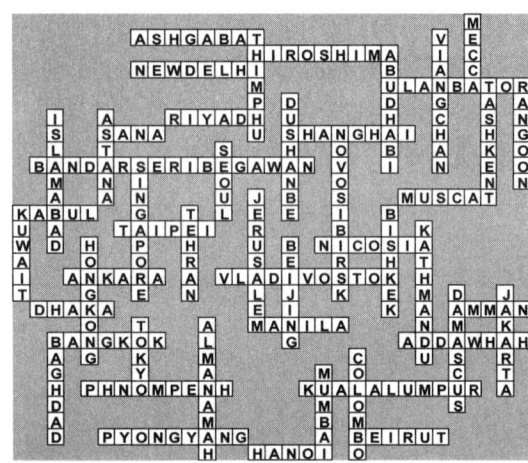

Asia: Physical Features (p. 53)
1. Urals
2. Gobi
3. Mekong
4. Arabian
5. Eastern Ghats
6. Yangtze
7. Karakum
8. Zagros
9. Borneo
10. Chukchi
11. Indus
12. Caspian Sea
13. Himalayas
14. Euphrates
15. Sri Lanka
16. Dasht-e Kavir
17. Western Ghats
18. Great Indian Desert
19. Baykal
20. Huang
21. Elburz
22. Takla Makan
23. Malay
24. Tigris
25. Hindu Kush
26. Indian
27. Dead Sea
28. Ganges
29. Rub'al Khali
30. Tien Shan

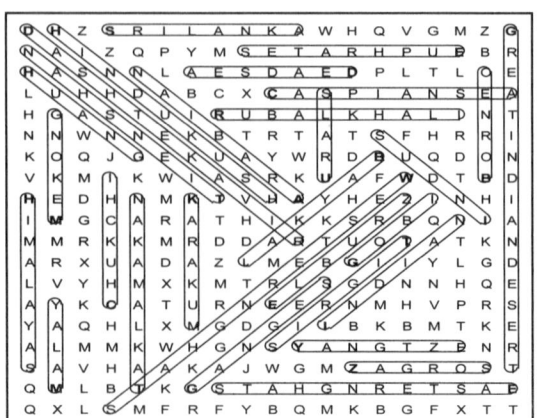

Asia: Plants, Animals, and Resources (p. 55)

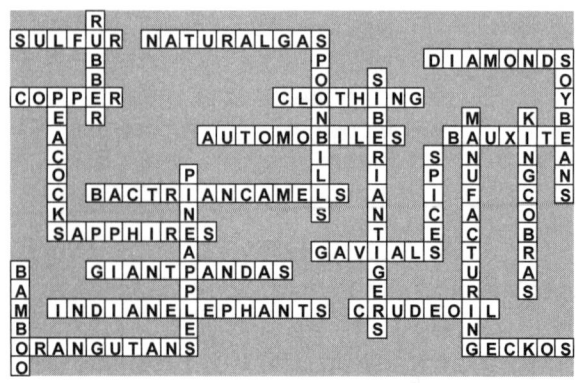

Asia: Population Density (p. 56)
1. 8.4
2. 136.1
3. 328.6
4. 5.6
5. 13.5
6. 126.1
7. 46.2
8. 337.2
9. 26.3
10. 302.2

From left to right on graph: Japan, India, Israel, China, Indonesia, Afghanistan, Laos, Saudi Arabia, Russia, Kazakhstan

Asia: Regions (p. 57)
1. SOUTHEAST ASIA
2. TROPICAL RAIN FOREST
3. SOVIET UNION
4. SUBCONTINENT
5. MIDDLE EAST
6. SIBERIA
7. TIBET
8. SOUTH ASIA
9. HOLY LAND
10. FAR EAST

Australia and Oceania: Locations of Major Cities (p. 58)

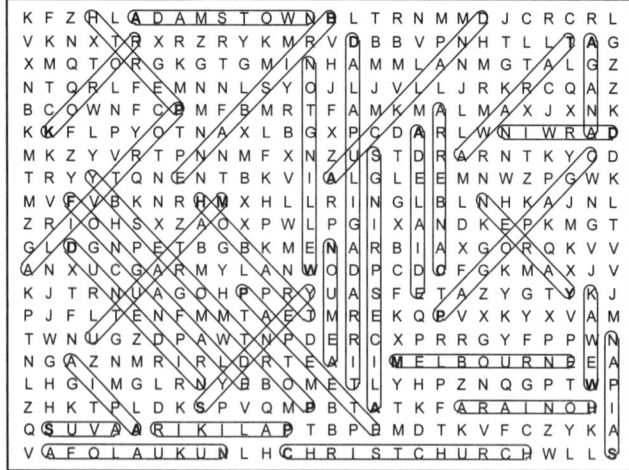

These coordinates are approximate.
Accept reasonable answers.
1. 24°S, 128°W
2. 35°S, 139°E
3. 13°N, 144°E
4. 24°S, 134°E
5. 14°S, 172°W
6. 37°S, 175°E
7. 27°S, 153°E
8. 35°S, 149°E
9. 43°S, 173°E
10. 7°N, 171°E

World Geography Puzzles — Answer Keys

Australia and Oceania: Locations of Major Cities (cont.) (p. 58)

11. 12°S, 131°E
12. 46°S, 171°E
13. 8°S, 179°E
14. 43°S, 147°E
15. 9°S, 159°E
16. 7°N, 134°E
17. 13°S, 176°W
18. 38°S, 145°E
19. 22°S, 167°E
20. 21°S, 174°W
21. 14°S, 170°W
22. 7°N, 158°E
23. 17°S, 149°W
24. 32°S, 116°E
25. 10°S, 147°E
26. 17°S, 168°E
27. 15°N, 145°E
28. 19°S, 178°E
29. 34°S, 151°E
30. 1°N, 173°E
31. 41°S, 175°E
32. 3°S, 143°E
33. 0°, 167°E

Australia and Oceania: Physical Features (p. 59)

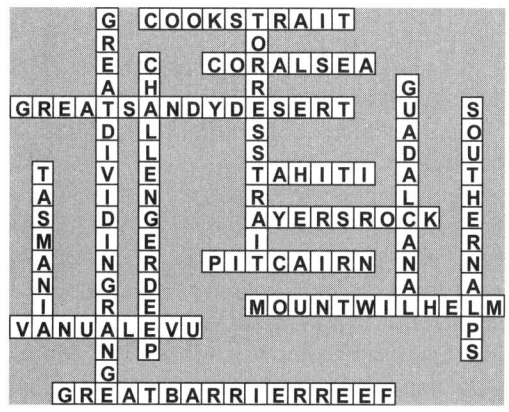

Australia and Oceania: Plants, Animals, and Resources (p. 60)

1. COPRA
2. MARSUPIAL
3. EUCALYPTUS
4. NICKEL
5. FISHING
6. GOLDEN WATTLE
7. AGRICULTURE
8. KOOKABURRA
9. OPALS
10. WOOL
11. KIWI
12. PLATYPUS
13. COPPER
14. TOURIST
15. KANGAROO

Australia and Oceania: Movement of Early People and Culture (p. 63)

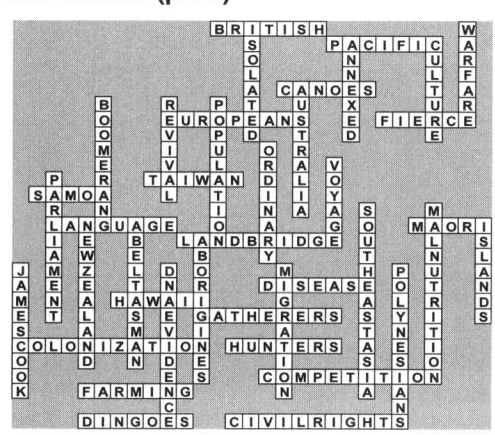

Australia and Oceania: Regions (p. 64)

3 Largest Countries: Australia, Papua New Guinea, New Zealand

Melanesia: Bismarck Archipelago, Solomon Islands, Vanuatu, New Caledonia, Fiji

Micronesia: Northern Mariana Islands, Federated States of Micronesia, Marshall Islands, Gilbert Islands (Kiribati), Nauru, Palau, Guam

Polynesia: Tonga, Western Samoa, American Samoa, Cook Islands, French Polynesia, Pitcairn Islands, Niue, Phoenix Islands (Kiribati), Tuvalu, Hawaiian Islands (USA, due to the ethnicity of the people more than the geographic location)

Antarctica: Locations (p. 65)

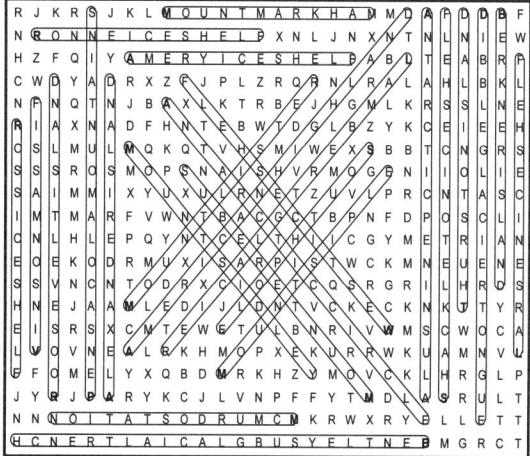

These coordinates are approximate. Some may be a range of coordinates or the coordinates may be for the center of the physical feature. Accept reasonable answers.

1. 72°S, 70°W
2. 73°S, 75°E (center)
3. 68°S to 74°S, 63°W to 82°E
4. 66°33"S
5. 70°S, 65°W (center)
6. 80°S, 115°W
7. 79°S, 49°W
8. 65°S, 135°E
9. 72°S, 68°W (center)
10. 66°S, 62°W (center)
11. 78°S, 166°E
12. 77°S, 167°E
13. 78°S, 162°E
14. 82°S, 161°E
15. 77°S, 126°W
16. 73°S, 126°W
17. 84°S, 50°W (center)
18. 75°S to 80°S, 50°W to 65°W
19. 79°S, 162°W
20. 78°S to 86°S, 115°W to 160°E
21. 66°S, 100°E (center)
22. 90°S, 0°
23. 73°S, 100°W
24. 78°S, 85°W
25. 74°S, 105°W (center)

Antarctica: Physical Features (p. 66)

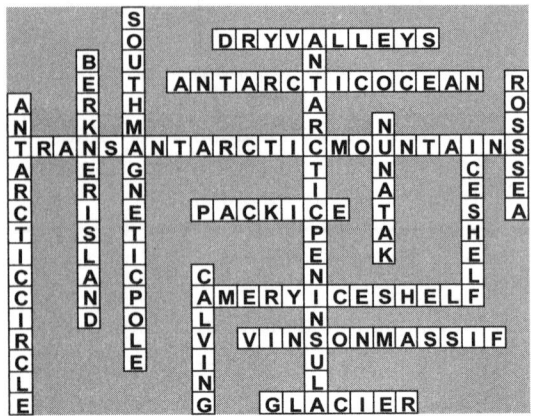

Antarctica: Plants and Animals (p. 67)

climate, organisms, bacteria, pearlwort, Seaweed, Krill, fish, penguins, emperor, albatross, Arctic tern, cormorant, leopard, Weddell, fur seal, baleen, humpback, killer, orca, dolphin

Antarctica: Exploration (p. 68)

1. ARISTOTLE
2. TERRA AUSTRALIS INCOGNITA
3. JAMES COOK
4. BELLINGSHAUSEN
5. JOHN DAVIS
6. WEDDELL SEA
7. ICE SHELF
8. SOUTH POLE
9. AMUNDSEN
10. SHACKLETON

Antarctica: International Agreements and Possible Resources (p. 70)

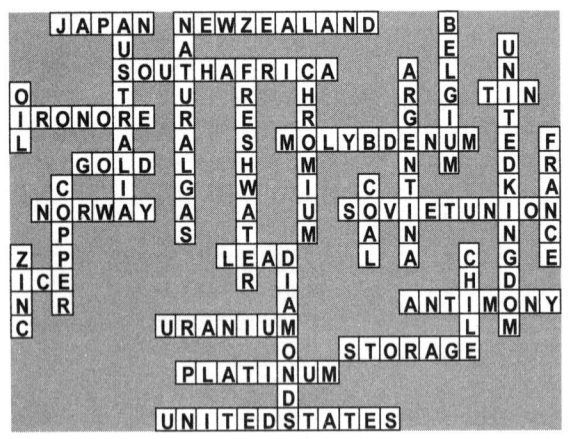

Bibliography

"Africa: Conflicts Without Borders." *ReliefWeb.* 10 Nov. 2008. Humanitarian Information Unit, U.S. Department of State. 18 Nov. 2009. <http://www.reliefweb.int/re/reb.nsf/db900SID/JOPA-7LDBRF?OpenDocument>

"Antarctica." *Encyclopaedia Britannica.* 2009. Encyclopedia Britannica Online. 7 Dec. 2009. <http://www.britannica.com/EBchecked/topic/27068/Antarctica>

"Antarctica." *Net Industries.* 2009. Net Industries. 7 Dec. 2009. <http://science.jrank.org/pages/397/Antarctica.html>

"Darfur Refugees." *Amnesty International USA.* 2009. Amnesty International USA. 18 Nov. 2009. <http://www.amnestyusa.org/darfur/darfur-facts/darfur-refugees/>

Kramme, Michael. (2002–2003) *Continents of the World Geography* series. *(Exploring Asia, Exploring Africa, Exploring Europe, Exploring South America, Exploring North America, Exploring Antarctica, Exploring Australia).* Quincy, IL: Mark Twain Media/Carson-Dellosa Publishing LLC.

Shireman, Myrl. (2003) *Discovering the World of Geography* series. Quincy, IL: Mark Twain Media/Carson-Dellosa Publishing LLC.

Stange, Mark, and Rebecca Laratta. (2002) *World Geography.* Quincy, IL: Mark Twain Media/Carson-Dellosa Publishing LLC.

Wax, Emily. "A Loss of Hope Inside Darfur Refugee Camps." *The Washington Post.* 30 Apr. 2006. The Washington Post. 18 Nov. 2009. <http://www.washingtonpost.com/wp-dyn/content/article/2006/04/29>